T0365362

The Story Never Ending

WHO me...who me? who's my guidance

The Author biography

HENNI HIDAYATI SUPARDI

To order additional copies of this book, contact:
Xlibris
0800-443-678
www.xlibris.co.nz
Orders@ Xlibris.co.nz

Scriptures taken from New Revised Standard Version Bible,
copyright © 1989, Division of Christian Education of the
National Council of the Churches of Christ in the United
States of America. Used by permission. All rights reserved.

ISBN: Softcover   978-1-5434-9567-6
       Hardcover   978-1-5434-9593-5
       EBook   978-1-5434-9566-9

Print information available on the last page

Rev. date: 10/26/2019

This a book talks about the Soul the spiritual
The soul and the spiritual. They're born in one body
Now they of body This book will describe
How the soul and how the spiritual
collaborate together.
In one born body the soul had role
In one body the spiritual had role

This book is all about my life experience. I believe among you and you thence I, myself. We aren't the same life experience. I like out to supernatural therefore I of life experience. This all about life experience. We had our living lifes. They aren't all peoples like acknowledges the supernatural living spirit I encourage the audient, shall read shall sees. What are shape or form inside supernatural? read my guidance are message...they just like shape had above earth on earth thence affect and impact our living earth thence impacting our life.

Oh, yea I will describing bit about all the illus I had dedicate on the pages. My guidance is seeing all the illus on illusion the form is similarity happen in author's life.

Who me…who me?
Who's my guidance
Migrant to Australia
NSW Campbelltown
Home sweet home
The house warmer
Aftermath house warmer

WHO ME?
I Henni

Who me; I describing who me? Oh, my mother's give me birth as infant body…thence god's give me the soul into body hail yea I the soul I of body thus I alive soul inside my body…thence my parent gives me, my birth name. My birth name is Henni this my first name.

I Henni I the soul I of body; My roles I carried all my muscles.

I carried all my bones. I responsible soul. I must eat well I must drink well. I isn't like weigh I isn't light obesity

I Henni I the soul I of body; I healthy soul I choice my nutrition I choice my fluid intake thus my body's health and happy

I Henni I the soul I of body; I amicably soul. I like peoples I like helps peoples as sick peoples as sick children as poor peoples.

I grievance soul I do everything and thinks. I work six days a week hue these are, heavy load. I grievance I hatred I tired I bore

I the soul I dedicate soul I of body. I like beautiful thing in me. I like changing wears in me. I like smell jasmine in me, I like smell roses in me. I like lavender in me I like perfume I like beautiful make up in me.

I Henni I the soul I of body; I enthusiastic soul I like driving I like gardening I like do food shopping. I like see field to field I like study I like walking at beach. I enthusebe soul I like dance I like tradition clothes I like watching movies I like music. I like going out with friend I like holiday with friend with family. I like eating out with friend. I like picnic with family and friends

I Henni I the soul I of body; I motivation soul I like seeking goal to goal. I like seeking skill to skill. I like seeking new experience I like learning new think and thing.

I Henni I the soul I of body; I like thinks I like do things but I nervous thus I cite I inter-independent soul. I was not born alone I did heard voices inside me ostensibly female voices. Myself ask "who Is she? is she my supporter? is she my guidance? Is she my friend? Is she my spiritual Is she born with me?

I henni I the soul I of body; I home soul. I choice my home object I good with that. I dedicate it well and bright I dedicate it all interesting ranks as color as qualities. I of perspective soul I Like green I like white I like blue I like pink

I henni I the soul I of body; I of atmosphere soul I like peace I like justice I like faith I like pious I like the comfortable. I nurse soul I like clean home I like clean car I like clean environment I like clean air thus it I healthy. I nurse soul I calm I patient I smart I cares

I Henni I the soul I of body; I creativity soul I like sawing I like art I like photos I like picture. I education soul I like study I achieve my certificate to certificate Am I miraculous achievement?

I Henni I the soul I of body; I mother soul. I love my children.

I educate them well. I enjoyed having them. I teach them. I tell them "what to do" right and just. I Magnanimous soul. I am listening I kind

I concern I heed I gift I bless. I direct to safe I direct to success

I Henni I the soul I of body; I holy soul I miraculous I see thing I heard thing why I heard voices above? The voice said We great you We shelter you. I respect full soul. I respect I polite I good manner

I Henni I the soul I of body; I belief soul I like candle I like herbal I like flower I like incense I like aroma salt I like aroma oil I like aroma tea I like aroma fruit.

I Henni I the soul I of body; I like culture. I like religion I religion soul. I like to pray I like rosary I like bible. I' Am catholic religion

WHO ME?

I the spiritual I am describing Who me oho my mother gives me birth I spirit I cite spiritual I born in one body. phooey I of body. my parent gives my birth name. My birth name is Hidayati. I the middle name after my body soul name…. I spiritual I Hidayati I confess I born I wasn't alone… I born with one body with one soul.

I the spirit cite I the spiritual I confess I body's spiritual I isn't settle spiritual. I like going out from my body I like out to supernatural.

I Hidayati, I the spiritual; I like out to supernatural I like visible things. Thereout I saw the tree the flower oho tensibly they had spirit. They cite tree of spirit They cite flower of spirit.

I Hidayati; I like out to supernatural I like hearing the tree voices the flower voices I like choice the voices Oh which and which I can trust? I saw the tree I saw the flower Myself asked are they healing tree? Are they healing flower?

I Hidayati I the spiritual; I like out to supernatural I like visibly the earth I like hearing the earth voices why the earth facetious with the trees? Why the earth facetious with the flower? Myself asked are they the spirit healing? or are they the spirit commotion?

I Hidayati I the spiritual; I like out to supernatural I like hearing the sky voices. I like seeing the shape the color the form the color I like think Is its bad shape bad voices. Are its good shape good voices?

Oh, why abruptly sound bad voices as women voices as men voices!

I Hidayati I the spiritual; I like out to supernatural I like seeing spiritualism I see they had varied shape They'd vary forms Myself asked why are they leave their bodies? I like out to supernatural I like sees disease as form as shape My self-asked which and which we must more caution

I Hidayati I the spiritual; I like supernatural I like thinks I like seeing what are thing doing? I like out to supernatural seeing young spiritualism Why are they out from their bodies? I like out to supernatural I seeing old spiritualism Why are they out from their bodies? Are these cite magic are spiritualism? myself asked what are the differences within young and old spiritualism?

I like out to supernatural; I like to see the decease What shape are they? Are they many shapes? What are voices are they? I Like thinks I like sees which good decease which bad decease?

I Hidayati I the spiritual; I like out to supernatural I visible above had form had shape as knife as knife as gun as gun as stone as stone. Myself asked is its magic knife. Is its magic stone myself asked what are thing for? Whose are like acknowledge them? Whose believe upon it?

I Hidayati I the spiritual; I like my home supernatural Therein I like singing with my flower I like singing inside my children room. My song my voices do impacts my children aha the impact they are, sing with me. I like seen my children spiritualism.

I Hidayati I the spiritual; I like singing with them. I like supernatural therein I went and visited my children bodies are soul. I like checking their health if they're soul health. I like eating with them I like to see inside them Whose are with them. Why I seen had light inside them? Asif holy cross light as if holy cross bright

Lucky oh lucky I get guidance. They are, guide me they shelter me they answer me they cite to me. The light the bright Inside the children its children are god they born; they bless by its god.

I Hidayati I the spiritual; I like out to supernatural I see the tree. I heard I aghast the tree of voices as it talks about me, I heard the flower are voices as it talks about me. They voice aren't friendly.

I heard the tree aren't like me because I like seeking god are inspiration I guest because it, they aren't like me I thought too because they're can't temptation me. I heard the flower are voices They aren't like me because they can't temptation me. They aren't Like me engaging with god are inspiration Wow I curious?

I Hidayati I the spiritual; I curious upon the tree the flower. I heard, the tree the flower voices they aren't happy voices. I heard they voices like giving me bad temptation. They sound aren't friendly upon me. I think because they cannot temptation me. They aren't like god are inspiration come to me

I Hidayati I the spiritual; I like out to supernatural They're visibly me Indeed I was not alone. They saw me, they heard me. I was with guidance. They heard voices above called me the tree the flower as if curious upon me. They thought I go out from my body I want seeking new things new skill new problem.

Furthermore, about me I Hidayati I the spiritual; I like out to supernatural I like accepted the consequences phooey me oho the bizarre I heard the tree talking and talking the odd I heard the flower laugh and laughing. I heard the tree temptation all walking people all driving peoples thence happen people well doing thence happen people are accident.

I Hidayati; I was in supernatural I like seen my body's soul called my name I like seeing my body's soul screamed for me. I like seeing my body's soul Henni she is wondering where me. I in supernatural I like engaging with my body's soul she my Henni

I Hidayati I the spiritual; I said to my soul she Henni Here I am, I was not far from you Myself soon come back to you. I will tell you the problem here who's good who's bad

Yea Here I am. I your spiritual I awareness body's soul do need spiritual help. Body's soul does need spiritual supporter. Body's soul does need spiritual's encouragement Body's soul do need spiritual's friend I heard your grievance and grievance You wasn't like to be alone. Oh, lucky oh lucky my body's soul she born she had me.

I Hidayati I the spiritual; I current like out to supernatural. I like see down living earth I like see above the earth Why I saw the sky have shape have form?" I curious" myself asking whose alive up there.

I Hidayati the spiritual; I like out to supernatural I like to see miraculous thing and think. Who shape up there? I like sees miraculous alive. Is it the soul up there? I ask my guidance What is miraculous? What is the mercy? I asked my guidance: which and which the earth? and which and which the sky? sign life miraculous. Sign life the mercy. I like out to supernatural Oh lucky oh lucky I had guidance They said the blue vary blue earth on earth but had life's Good life as host life. The red fire earth on earth there its heaven hell have shape as from

I Hidayati I the spiritual; Oh, oh I said 'Life' in the blue! I baffled. I said alone I believe what I visibly I get impact by it. I alone visibly the blue earth I feel as if "thriller" the weather O it did impact my supernatural. I feel the weather I bit hotter. Therefore, I visible many peoples went to the beach When on blue earth appearing to live earth

I Hidayati I the spiritual; Lucky oh lucky I had guidance. They rapidly cover my head, cover my body as if my guidance They aren't shame inside me They aren't fear inside me. I the spiritual I like out to supernatural I visibly the sun I curious myself talks. I guest aren't all I visibly the sun the sun healthy sun, I saw today the sun as if can hurt me.

I called to my guidance I asked them. Why today the sun I visibly as if against me? lucky oh lucky I had guidance They above me They voices said today the sun it called decry sun. Today the sun called enemies sun Oh I baffled I dismay. I asked whose are bodies pray to the sun to the sun? Oh, I mused who it the sun? is it the sun cite belief I think yea! I caution I upon belief I caution I upon believer.

My Family AND BODY SOUL BODY SPIRITUAL

We confess on 1993 my husband my children and I We were immigrants from New Zealand to Australia. When we first arrived in Australia. Wow. We glee We visibles Australia really magnificent Country…We visibly Sydney NSW of maps. Therein had many marvelous cities…we of map therein we visible upon Sydney NSW chi we see in map Thereat we visible NSW Campbelltown we visible in map Campbelltown as if City.

We Abrupt we one day we went driven around to NSW Campbelltown. Thence we driven toward Narelle road We visible there Off Narrelan road there it had vary state are places wahoo …

I Henni; I and my husband we facetious we laugh. We both are visible on off Narrenlan Thereout we visible one a place it cited Current hill state. We visible it we proud we merry.

I Henni; I visibly the Current hill state I can see in here Oh this state massive current hill state I said to my husband I like the Current hill State Therein I visible have many are streets. I heard my husband He said he great the current hill state he's merry he's enthusebe.

I Hidayati I the spiritual; I said to my husband the perspective here most houses the houses seem very color full. I visible here or there every house is look very green. I visibly the grass the homeowner, good maintain. I guess the city council well maintain too the environment the road here looks clean, there look clean. I like clean road. My husband respond, isn't only the clean road I like to see. the traffic also my concern.

I Hidayati; hi henni, the street here or there, the homeowner good maintaining environment I visible the home environment I saw looks clean here and there

I Henni; yea hidaya I saw everywhere look tidy and green as if lovely sited on green grass. I said to my husband, I visibly yea! the Council worker they're maintain the environment really well. My husband responds "Oh you! You too desire"

I Hidayati;I said to my husband I like live here wahoo I like Current hill state. I visible on the morning the atmosphere here seems quiet.

I shall visible on afternoon time or on nighttime Yea hopefully aren't busy aren't hectic. My husband responds oh you! oh hectic You always think about superstition.

I Henni; Yea hopefully not, the perspective here aren't bizarre I am concern toward the traffic. Oh, I believe on the morning seem okay wow see on afternoon or on night I guest differences I heard my husband respond. He said "ah different" ah you who you! I hatred hearing superstition thing and thinks. Is it you the create the creator think the superstition think"?

I Hidayati; I respond to my husband I said, "who you who me!" "you are as if" "I is the fact" however I like Current hill state the environment as look as enthusiastic for me for Henni. I visible our children, they will enthusebe if we live here. I feel I merry live here I saw the perspective the atmosphere safe for me safe for my children. My husband responds yea.yea fare oh fare for you as I wasn't always work in Sydney

I Henni; I think on the morning if I walks here, I'll fear. I still new here. Yea I fear bit. Yea I enthusebe walking but not alone.

On the morning the road very, quiet I guest all people are working the children and the children They I guest all at school.

The perspective on morning I felt I bit bright my energy up. I can walk but…? Am I safe here?

I Henni; I facetious with my husband I said aha shall we stop the car by Current Hill road I visible oh currenthill road such as long road Wow the perspective here or there many tree I guest on summer time the tree are for shades My husband respond oh these tree aren't concern

I Hidayati; I saw there off current hill road. My husband and I We visibly there it had one was, magnificent street. This street cites Thomas way street Oh lucky oh lucky! we visible one land of Thomas street.

I Henni; my husband and I we said oho see one live for us oh it seems enormous a land. Wow we're merry We enthusebe We cite we're benediction thence we laugh we great this land My husband said oh lucky oh lucky we had a one land live for us. I respond Oh fortune oh fortune This land for us

I Hidayati; "Oh it benefits oh will be fortune" we shall can build massive home on this land it will look fortune.

I heard inside me above me They been facetious Oh I don't aghast who's facetious inside me or above me. I believe they my guidance they my fortune they my goal

I Hidayati; They're can see this land and they just. They're can think how to build how to design. I benediction upon my guidance They sound they're like the land They're sound wahoo to the land I heard them merry. I proud I merry having them inside me above me.

I Henni I the spiritual; Oho yea henni. I heard our guidance They said: hail yea buys it! build it! this good are fortune for us. I heard I merry I great them. I think they can creator the design for our new home aha lucky oh lucky we of them. My husband abruptly responds oh...oh...your superstition tells you oh hidaya....?

I Henni; Oh, lucky oh lucky I born with my spiritual. I visible she been invited many friends inside me. I wonders why me dedicate I was so faith full. I day by day I see myself phooey…

I Henni I the spiritual; I thanks to our guidance. I do need friend with me inside me. I do need supporter with me inside me Oh aghast oh aghast I curious my husband looked different toward me

I Henni; oh you don't curious toward him, lets him free We do need god are spirit They choice the land for us thence we bought it This the first land We build our first home at Thomas way street I said to my husband. Shall we driving further toward current hill road What perspective can we see from here from there?

I Henni; I and my husband, we visible from Current hill state We saw the sign the KFC and the MC Donal tensibly it just isn't far from our home street. Yea it handy if I lazy cooking. We just driving there Only take 2-minute driving from our street, we get there. See It just close from our address

I Henni; I visibly The KFC if I lazy cooking, we will go there We are eating out. lucky oh lucky our street isn't far from KFC from MC Donald.Yea we enthusebe I said, I merry if I lazy doing cooking Thereout very handy There are KFC there had MC Donald tensibly it both are close to our home street.

I can visibly our Children's too They enthusebe. Wah I did hear my children They are voices They been glee, they been jubilant I heard their voices called my name, but I laugh I ignore them.

I heard their voices facetious toward each other's They said shall we shall we. eating out thereout had KFC thereat had MC Donald tensibly these enjoyable KFC and MC Donald aren't far from our home this will merry us

I heard my children said see here enthusebe, shall we tell mum, shall we go there…wahoo we can eating out, we great mum oh she don't have to cook for us KFC and Mc donal, we merry with that…it full filled us aha what ha mum ha for.

I the spiritual I of body; I visible I heard aha my children oh my children You aren't think well toward healthy site. I heard they facetious they said aha thankfulness we live here, we lucky the KFC and MC Donald it close but…? but…? our mum she wasn't enthusiastic toward it

I the spiritual; hail yea the children ah children I must think I must do what my guidance said the children yea children They can make They own consideration

I heard they said shall we asking Dad driving or walking us there to KFC to MC Donald oh he seems easy and easy going than mum was.

Aha going with him enjoyable Shall we encouraging him going out eating out there KFC and there its MC Donald aha we like it

I Henni and I Hidayati; Occasional is okay oh see today seem on afternoon if we can eat KFC here I shall I informing our guidance We trust in them shall we hearing their perspective? If it okay, we buy it for today afternoon lucky oh lucky if today, we can eat out.

I Hidayati the spiritual; I shall inform them I believe on them They more caution than me than my soul henni Oh dear my guidance sees today our children asking for Mc Donald and KFC

tensibly my children said today eating out better than eating at home oho my guidance aha is it okay for today afternoon eating out?

We holy holy spirit; wow…dear Henni oh dear hidaya We heard too our children voices They been facetious about KFC about MC Donald Ooh thereout we saw we mused we baffling this afternoon the supernatural bit thriller Wow KFC or MC Donald we mused today…today afternoon KFC and MC Donald part are supernatural superstition oho today afternoon the supernatural around us therein We see spiritualism as bad as seitan walking spirit oho dear today afternoon very superstition

We holy holy spirit; we visibly the spiritualism, they in supernatural. They cite magic spiritualism. They also cite supernatural walking spirit bad spirit. They wind wind but they just like disease wind wind. In supernatural They're doing as bad as seitan doing oho can happen You all get sick tummy

We angel we said; we visible oho today afternoon the supernatural as if aren't healthy The magic wind spiritualism oho they are around you all They want eating with you They bad temptation they bad influence Caution Oh dear can happen you all get tummy problem thus today afternoon you all can't eating out

I Hidayati; Ooh tell me my guidance where are they? around my body? I can't hear them Shall I going out from my body I shall see them oho why I can't out from my body if I inside body I can't hear as voices jubilant I can't hear hectic around me

We saint host; hail dear my Henni my Hidayati They aren't far from you Wow dear today Thursday on afternoon this wasn't good afternoon The weather also appeared red earth it appeared cloud earth Therein many wind wind are spirit there up had shape as magic lion magic tiger magic leopard

We holy holy spirit; The magic spiritualism They here they'd around my girl body They'd around my children bodies We visible they magic are spiritualism They great if the weather cloud or read as fire on earth. The spiritualism they like it. Their bodies pray toward the earth above We visible the spiritualism they called the shape tiger lion to fellow to living earth thence visited our home.

We heard we visible within spiritualism and spiritualism They like facetious with the shape lion leopard or tiger. They are collaborate they're like temptation as if the temptation for our girl for our children O we aware!, there are bad about spiritualism There are good about spiritualism Caution they like eating with you, eating with our children Caution they aren't all like you live here thus you caution we caution see ah, today afternoon aren't good afternoon for you all eating KFC or MC Donald here

I Henni I the soul; I said yea my guidance oh okay oh yea find by me I'll safe my money.

I Hidayati; O dear my Henni wow isn't easy you said that instead you still have to do the cooking for them

I Henni; yea dear my guidance my hidaya Yea find by me as long as they are peace and merry with your loves.

I Holy spirit; yea dear yea dear Oh live them to me They of mind they're will peace. Oh, go oh go you. You's move on and see You still have time.

I Hidayati; shall we visible others perspective What else…?we can visible further more inside Current hill state.

I see oh see thereat Current hill's Park ground wahoo it close from our Thomas way street I visible very enthusebe for our children.

I Henni; We shall see this park ground if it safe for the children to claim up to claim down hi I see the grass also here look healthy as green I think we safe we sited on picnic here.

I Henni; Oh, I merry live here Thereout our children, they will enthusiastic Inside park ground They can ride here, they can ride there. aha we also can visible our home address from here wahoo the children will enthusiastic on afternoon They're will enjoyed came here

We angel angel; Oh, dear henni Oh dear Hidayati be aware upon background are supernatural Here aren't every afternoon safe oho fall down or fight can happen it happen. We see park ground's supernatural do happen bad on afternoon.

We seen within spiritualism and spiritualism They like going into children of bodies They are riding faster They're claim and claim We seen the spiritualism as the wind as seitan They like going inside children body make problem Caution on afternoon time.

We angel angel; thereat visible Thereat had magic lion magic tiger fellow from the earth to living earth thence fell inside the park ground they saw our children They knew here if they don't like them. Magic lion magic tiger They wind are can going inside your children thus can burn the children body 'soul body 'spiritual thus our children mood abruptly changing as emotional or they aren't listening to the parent.

Oh, See Henni oh see Hidayati, the background's supernatural still safe on the morning than the afternoon. there are on the morning the spirit the shape isn't the same

I Hidayati; wow fear me why henni and I We aren't thinks the sign danger Ooh we sorry we had weak mind. Oh, benefit oh benefit having guidance I heard you invoke Your words indeed I following I heard you invoke Oh my children safe from accident as fall as incident as riding Thank you oh thank you, my guidance my shelter. You just, you are my direction You safe my children Your word outright mercy Oh safe my children from bad spirit from bad luck bad day.

I Henni; hi hidaya, shall we move on We see other perspective what more we can visible from here Oh see on Current hill road Thereat had bus stop. Occasionally we do need bus. wahoo handy the bus. The bus stop isn't far from Thomas way street Aha lucky me. I don't need the car every day dropping my children to their school. aha I will teach them how to catch the bus. See they will happy. Therein bus they are meeting with their new are friend This be enthusebe for them

We angel angel; oh, dear Henni oh dear Hidayati Oh caution heed supernatural are spirit in the bus can pushing, can fighting happen can happen inside the bus. The problem can arise from bus of bad spirit Oh visible inside the bus had bad spiritualism They invisible. they wind spirit They invisible they can go inside children to children.

They're can temptation the children to hit to fight pushing It can happen your children get hurt. Oh, happen can happen. There is safe day There are bad day

Oh, Henni we visibly you. Oh, Henni nothing wrong with your car. Your spiritual can drive them to school day by day this your spiritual role. Yea isn't fare for you to all do. What A spiritual A for Spiritual is, to help you to assist you

I Hidayati ; wow yea certainly I will do! I drive my children to school Yea I heed them They my concern. They my worry. I visibly we live here outright different compare We lived in New Zealand. I see in new zealand Henni was, enthusiastic driven them to school but here she's demanding on me

We angel angel; O dear Henni, oh dear Hidayati Caution

Thereout we visibles your home supernatural visiting by spiritualism Thereout They of bodies They peoples Indonesian live here. They peoples are garud They people are banten We visibles we aghast They are, your friends and your husband of friend.

We visible they're as if your enemies We curious Why they body of spiritualism They out from their bodies thence like visited your home We saw them. This aren't good sign for your home Oh can happen your home lost fortune Oh can happen your children aren't doing well at school

I saint host; I heard you, yea I believe what you see. There I was I visibles the Hadis earth the mujarobat earth Those are, I visibly engaging upon bodies of soul I see them I heard them They people are garut Yea they people are banten I guess they my girl' husband his friend. I visibly them I knew acknowledge them These are friend They very danger friend sees upon my girl.

I saint host; I visibly they very envious upon my girl's dedicate here. Ooh worry me Oh sorry me I visibes my children they smart children Asif can happen bad spiritualism They're can impact my children are goal oh angel I do concern upon my girl and her husband "happiness" Ooh dear What shall I do? I must think furthermore what option I should do?

Holy holy cross light earth; hail saint I heard your grievance. About jin jin wind men of bewhiskeret. Yea saint did not your holy holy spirit investigation how the life here How the supernatural here hail saint visibly it! the supernatural here. Will happening…? O dear we visible we sorry for your girl. We mused see her supernatural

Holy cross light earth; We visible! we aghast Henni and Hidaya she'll get the bad supernatural Her's supernatural Therein arriving group are spiritualism They cite magic spiritualism are banten They cite magic spiritualism are garut We said they're group spiritualism seitan thus caution holy holy spirit! Can happen Henni and Hidaya she can get hurt by them.

Hail saint hail holy spirit People are garud people are banten they're lived here. They of belief they believer as magical as lion male tiger male leopard male. These cite are jin jin wind hell fire yea caution yea heed toward them We saw these males are jin jin wind hell fire. We seen they are, enemies toward women.They hatred upon her. They ferocious upon her. They went inside her. They're shucking or eating her hormone. Oh, she looked awful her motivation gone down

Holy holy cross; hail saint hail holy spirit See her, she become lazy she become obesity. she eats and eat she drink and drink thence her desire down her sexuality down. We watch her abruptly she hatred seeing men. She isn't enthusiastic facetious with men. We watch we heard we mused. The magic jin jin inside her telling her what to do. What is right only according to them oh wistfully oh wistfully we saw toward this woman.

She was beautiful one Yea many males they're willing to married her but her physical her mentality down by Islamic magic lion by magic tiger by magic leopard. Hail saint hail holy holy spirit yea heed them Do not let them visit your girl home supernatural. Happen can happen toward Henni toward Hidayati. She also had enemies here Hail dear saint however we did send our voices toward this awful woman We said hail dear talks to us hail dear talks to us Oho dear she can't hear us phooey she. We see she instead she over eating over drinking Further we turn our self to the north side

I Hidayati; oh, dear mother saint mother You all seem mused what are you hearing from father holy cross Oh dear mother saint You all seem disappointed oh dear mother oh dear holy spirit tells me what is going on….?

We saint We holy holy spirit; O dear Hidayati. We must acknowledge about people why peoples they abruptly obesity Why is that…?this can happen to anybody, but we are here to preventing this isn't happen upon Henni body and soul. We indeed we must heed we must stop it coming to Henni body and soul.

I Hidayati; tell me my mother saint is it because had that, had jinn wind are hell fire in supernatural. I can't go out to supernatural. Oho this isn't fare for me such as agonized I live here oh mother I heard obesity I mused and fear because what are…?

we saint saint ; oho dear Hidayati according to holy cross Here often appeared had bad wind from mujarobat earth God are visible garud and banten They like rosary to magic mujarobat therein magic lion tiger leopard thus the wind shape fly to living supernatural but they are, magic doing abruptly get into women thence mass her or wasted her life. According to god are holy cross It soon can happen to Henni to you Hidayati God are see your enemies also garud and banten. They're hazardous people live here

Holy cross; hail saint sees it. These spiritualisms they been guide by Islamic magic jin jin are wind men of bewhiskeret. Islamic magic jin wind jin mens They're tells the spiritualism to temptation Henni and Hidayati to leave her guidance further They're temptation Henni to leave her home then they're temptation Henni there are holy men there are better men for the children

I saint I holy spirit; Oh, hurt me lord O lord we aren't worry Hidayati already see her future. Henni she easy gets temptation by Hidayati Yea lord by we teach by we bless Current Hidayati she is, in the high holy living thence she already saw the future living. Truth lord by our teaching Hidayati she high holy spiritualism than spiritualism is garud than spiritualism is banten

Holy holy cross; Well saint we will see your teaching method will safe. Well holy spirit we will see your teaching method will safe. we see the improvement Hidayati how she will fly up, we'll hearing Hidayati voices pray how she get into us.

Holy cross light earth bright earth; We visibly the magic spiritualism They're been guide they're been shelter by Hadis earth by mujarbat earth of magic jin wind jin men of bewhiskeret by Iblis Iblis wind women dress in white We hearing they're collaborate to hurt Henni to hurt Hidayati Caution saint Caution holy spirit Your girl we choice for us.

mused oh mused Islamic magic they are, jin jin wind men of bewhiskeret They wishing bad upon Henni's married They wishing bad upon Henni's goal Magic Jin wind jin men of bewhiskeret They wishing bad upon Henni fortune They of magic lion magic tiger magic leopard those cite are jin jin wind hell fire. Caution these are hazardous Oh thriller oh thriller for Henni live here Oh thriller for the children live here Oh dear holy holy spirit You all caution! Yea shelter Henni Yea shelter Hidayati. The magic lion magic tiger magic leopard tensibly they soon will against Henni they'll against Hidayati against you all holy holy spirit They're hatred visibly Henni had guidance host.

We angel angel; Yea god We visibly them We followed them thence we described them upon saint saint. Upon holy holy spirit. Hail yea God. We investigated from above. We visible bodies are spiritualism They often they're out from their bodies Thence we saw they're collaborate with magic tiger magic lion magic leopard. After that we saw, they go down as bad wind bad visited into Henni's home supernatural. Mused oh mused we saw They're together they're watched How henni doing They're watched how you all shelter Henni how you all shelter Hidaya

We angel angel; We visible the spiritualism They Islamic believer but we saw They aren't the same believer as others Islamic believer live here. They had spiritualism cite they're magic spiritualism They're like supernatural What we already visible, we believe they bodies are souls They people are magic. Oh, phooey people are garud oh phooey people are banten They're old men they're old women

We visible they rosary as if for bad aiming Just only for Henni just only for Hidayati. Tensibly only people are garud People are banten they Henni're enemies lives here. They magic cite magic killing magic are supernatural We heard. We aghast we aghast They're rosary aiming for Henni's married break up. Oh, sad oh sad We still visibly the old men with his family collaborate with the old women're family. Oh, only to against Henni against Hidayati to get her married break up

Angel said; The old men the old women They indeed henni enemies They indeed Hidayati enemies. We cite to saint we cite to holy spirit Caution we visibles vary jin jin wind men of bewhiskeret We visibly Iblis Iblis Iblis are wind women dress in white dress in black They winds are magic. They are wind, can going inside Henni's body thence if they get the knife, they can kill Henni's body. It can happen! To henni

Angel said; We saw people are garud People are banten live here lived in Australia. They're pray they rosary upon Hadis earth upon mujarobat earth Oh we saw the earth earth tensibly had magic belief These beliefs are working for to kills. Indonesian within Indonesian peoples for example Indonesian poor are living here. They envious upon Indonesian rich are living here. See it thus will happen upon Henni life here

Angel angel said; Phooey Islamic people are garud here Phooey Islamic people are banten here. They believe upon belief as magic jin jin are wind men of bewhiskeret Jin jin wind hell fire they are, magic lion tiger leopard They believe upon magic Iblis Iblis are wind These are winds They can going inside human bodies They also cite they are, seitan wind they bad wind They shape we see cat bird dog they're colour black and red as fire They colour white and white They can two form as human wind as cat cat wind They magic wind Magic kill magic defect magic torment O lord we cite to the saint to the holy holy spirit Caution heed Henni heed Hidaya.

I Angel; hail saint hail holy spirit See Islamic Jin jin wind Iblis Iblis wind They like spiritualism They making magic are spiritualism We saw jin jin are wind men of bewhiskeret They like bodies're souls they're like spiritualism. They teach are spiritualism how to backbite peoples within peoples How to challenge people within people caution oh heed henni oh heed hidaya

I angel; hail saint oh see This can happen to henni. See her See the husband Why they're sudden fight for no reason? See her why sudden she distrusts oh she dislikes this can happen within she with her Hidayati within she with holy holy spirit Caution and heed her

We angel; we saw we heard Jin wind jin men They of roles for bodies of spiritualism They must out from their bodies and live in supernatural oh danger Yea warns for you Caution heed and heed Hidayati We visibly jin jin men are doing We curious! Further, we visible body of spiritualism They like jin jin are role We visible They like lives in supernatural We saw the spiritualism They adore are jin jin of magic lion magic tiger magic leopard the spiritualism they're proud of them. We visible in supernatural the spiritualism They work for voodoo and vice

We holy holy spirit; oh, angel angel, baffled oh baffled yea thriller oh thriller We heard your information oh yea this rare we heard in New Zealand where we lived. Certainly, we caution we mused oh rapidly we heed Hidayati We are her supporter See ah Henni and Hidayati She our bright one. She our honest one. She our light one Why she mischance here.

We holy holy spirit; We confess we love live here We did saw our girl are goal better here We did saw our children are goal achieve here We never thought We had enemies here

We angel angel; Ooh holy holy spirit. Current your girl have home She cannot see when the bad coming We are, certain curious Why your home been watch full by Islamic Hadis earth of magic belief by Islamic mujarobat earth of magic belief. This bizarre, we are curious

We holy holy spirit; hail yea angel we curious too oh bizarre people are garud lives here Yea odd odd people are banten live here. Lucky ah lucky our girl Henni and Hidayati She like our advice she rapidly listening She easy calm She easy fear She easy changing

We saint; yea lucky ah lucky we of her She like learning She believe our belief as aroma She adore it; she praises it She like skill She like seeking experience

We angel; well done holy holy spirit well teaching Yea we will seeing up there What still going on up there. We will see we will tell you soon if bad happen or good happen We see you again…?

Holy holy cross earth; hail saint hail holy holy spirit, current lives here Henni and Hidayati "caution" can happen can sudden your girl get mischance get bad luck by magic are spiritualism We saw they collaborate with jin jin men of bewhiskeret with Iblis Iblis are win women dressing in white or black.

Caution heed Henni oh heed Henni's bedroom Oh heed Henni clothes Caution holy holy spirit Oh heed Henni shoes caution heed Henni make up We visible spiritualism are garud They're magic spiritualism They are aiming They will do magic toward Henni belonging

We holy holy spirit; yea lord, sad oh sad us Thank you for you invoke your information We heed we help Henni We also caution oh seem these issues are very comment in current are life. These people are garud They like supernatural games People are banten They like supernatural games. Yea lord we want leave Henni we want leave Hidayati we caution We will be teaching Hidayati toward our belief how to curse off them.

We holy holy spirit; Hail saint saint, what are option do we have? The belonging of Henni. As are thing going to be magic What shall we do? hi angel tell us Oh holy cross tells us Oh hail saint

saint what are procedure for magic. Hoo we did heard spiritualism are voices inside our bathroom They're converses They like our home, but they are…? They aware they saw We visible them. They're very envious upon Henni expensive things They envious toward Henni She can cook They envious upon Henni's love toward her children

We holy holy spirit; Therefore caution our girl toward buying toward eating out Yea the angel said They parent They aren't cares upon body of spiritualism We think they're been neglecting their children are spiritualism We now coherent See they aren't happy spiritualism we caution Yea had bad about them There are good about them but they are, still hazardous

Holy holy cross earth; Hail yea Holy holy spirit We cite the bad about the spiritualism We visibly they adore magic lion magic tiger magic leopard We visible the spiritualism They also like collaborate with them.

We holy holy spirit; The bad about the spiritualism They inform and inform They lets their bodies knowing thing new to them They're envy how Henni, she doing? how he doing? The bad about them They can going inside our children bodies They are, the spiritualism They like influence and influence to fight and fight They like malign and malign Oho can happen to our children thus they're fight and fight for aren't reason

We host angel; hail saint hail holy holy spirit heard us Therefore shelter your girl Your children We care also upon your girl She is alone here We heard her decease voices They been called our name They been called holy holy cross name for need shelter

They been called holy holy saint for need shelter thus we rapidly watching We above we saw the enemies Yea any time can happen magic happen We see people are garud live here They nasty they are jin jin men of whiskers They of animal spirit in fact as magic spirit as lion as tiger as leopard spirits These spirit are nasty spirit, hot spirit.

We holy holy spirit; wah why worry aren't time yet for us to challenge them We love our girl We love our children We own massive home We are merry we benediction People are garud Spiritualism are garud Spiritualism are banten They aren't like seeing we are happy Phooey garud phooey banten They aren't our problem We live here we want not creator the enemies We see our girl body's soul We saw she enthusiastic doing at home good fare on her.

Phooey Henni We saw she love baking We enjoy eating it We see she like learning We great her We see she is cooking nice food for her husband for her children We happy we bless her. Abruptly why we heard the magic spiritualism They hectic they said oh don't cook for him oh don't clean for him

We holy holy spirit; we do heard We did see our girl she enjoyed having children The spiritualism abrupt inside our home supernatural we heard They cry alone They wistfully alone We never heard our girl grievance We visibly she magnanimous mother The spiritualism they're shame They're hatred seeing her phooey spiritualism magic

We holy holy spirit; We seen them We do disappointed We visibly them inside our home supernatural We are blessing them abruptly they're screamed said and said fauk…fauk your blessing

We holy holy spirit; hail angel angel we do we kept Hidayati inside her's body We hatred seeing our home supernatural too superstition We heard abruptly Hidayati she is screaming alone She isn't settling spiritual inside body. Hail angel! we did we making Hidaya Goosebumps We said see and see the tree See and see the flower There are bad spirit come from the wind earth come from the wind sky They wind fall to our home supernatural The wind but form but shapeThey hotter wind they can burn Hidaya if Hidaya out to home supernatural

I Hidayati; wow I thought you all love me You all care about me Why you all close my ears my eyes my fore head These aren't fare you all doing toward me Wow about time you all hearing me screaming hearing me jumping inside my body I will do it I will isn't like you kept me in my body. I the spiritual I like supernatural watch me don't kept me inside if you do it I will scream hi come on..come on open the way for me I like out into my home supernatural I really like visited my children I love go out with them. I bore inside my body

Hidayati; O yea you all can have my henni I enjoy out to my supernatural I love singing with my children Am I lucky I have them? Oh, come on open the way for me! I will go out I will comeback if I want to comeback…?Oh my holy holy spirit I saw you all enjoyed my home You enjoy my body I isn't.

I the spiritual I Hidayati; oh having you're inside my body aha my guidance I can visibly my body She is bright she isn't need me every day but she do need holy holy spirit every day aha my guidance you are Henni's daily activities You are her helper Now you all here my guidance I can free choice Open it I out I out Good bye my guidance open the ways out for me I cry I screamed they aren't open the way out for me Why and why?

We holy holy spirit; We saw her, jump up jump down we laugh we laugh eventually we lets her see but only bit the outside like it We saw her aghast her dismay her disappointed thence we saw her She quiet alone We visibly her she did saw the supernatural odd and bizarre She think and think We heard she grievance She cite why and why this happen? She thinks alone she said alone We been visited by spiritualism, but they aren't person like me

We holy holy spirit; we heard Hidayati said wow yea I saw they pollution dash on earth wow she dismays we heard her called. She asked hail my guidance because of them. Your shut every way out for me wow why is that? Are they will burn me?

I Hidayati; I guess I must apologist to you all Oh lucky oh lucky I of holy holy spirit may I can reflect, what will happen without you all had inside me? I believe they can burn me burn me

I hidayati I like supernatural Why Goosebumps here? why thriller here? hail dear my holy holy spirit Why is it Goosebumps? why is it look thriller? I had knowledge I had skill I'd healing I certainly I can curse them Tell me whose them"? hail my guidance You high than me You all fly high than me You high see than me Tell me! what is going on inside my home?

I henni; Yes, tell me too my guidance Is this my home or is this geosphere home Wow we just build new home Why sudden happen? Hectic here Tell me my guidance where awry we doing!? I felt bit thriller inside my home am I abnormal?

I hidayati yea thriller henni yea I seen henni there bit, geosphere as if had form ostensibly they had shape oh aghast they are, pollution tensibly as wind dash, they are, hotter for me they can burn me. guidance I can't going out to supernatural I guest Only here I can't I always out In New Zealand my home supernatural

I Hidayati; In New Zealand I lived I always out to supernatural I guess my home supernatural there I get more blessing In New Zealand I out to supernatural I saw on the morning the sun sun have spirit as if have life inside it. I saw on the nigh I saw the star star I saw the nigh moon moon tensibly have life changing in it.

Hidayati; I like New Zealand I often get the mercy. I saw the holy saint moon the holy spirit moon They do moon. I saw angel moon moon They bright they light Am I miraculous spiritualism? I am inviting them comes into my home Oh lucky oh lucky me I lived In New Zealand I can invite them. Why here I mischance? Why here I hurt this just unfair

We holy holy spirit; Oh dear my hidaya we visible We sorry toward you We awareness you like your home supernatural, Just sudden happen bad coming The bad belief the bad spiritualism They been visited your home They aren't cool shape they different of temperature Therefore we shut off you's way out to our home supernatural Oh you don't said we mean upon you Indeed we aren't mean upon you We did it we concern if you get burn

I Hidayati; Hail my guidance yea I believe upon you I so baffled. Why they temperature hotter than me? I also wind I so human wind. I so cite body's spiritual I curious, why they are citing they my husband of friend? I baffling Why they spiritualism? They are hotter temperature than me.

Tell me! my guidance Are they good wind for me? Why I am different than them? Oh, lucky oh lucky I of guidance, they can visibly bad coming. They awareness I can get hurt. They can shut off my way out Oh now I awareness the concern. Yea I do need guidance help I isn't like hot temperature. wow what A guidance A for? They safe me they calm me down

We holy holy spirit; Oh, dear Hidayati oh dear. luck oh lucky hidaya she is, form healthy wind. Yea just she isn't hotter wind Oh see, we visible hidayati she was in supernatural She was bird wind She so human wind She of human voices She isn't bird voices Oh dear hidaya, we did consideration upon spiritualism, among them They of temperature. The temperature always come from bodies and souls.

We holy holy spirit; Bodies and soul They do need are making deed for their spiritualism. We visibly bodies and soul They people are garud They people are banten. They your husband of friends They are magic believer oh certainly they're spiritualism happen they are, as wind dash as wind polluted, they aren't enough doing deed

We holy holy spirit; We saw body and soul They pray upon magic lion magic tiger magic leopard These cite are sins Thus they spiritualism in supernatural They will get hotter temperature We heard body and soul They pray different pray than others Islamic believer. They pray we cite pray are sinners cite magic sinners They can hurt henni and hidaya

We holy holy spirit; aha therefore Hidayati now she quiet and she quiet. I think she dismay hoo now Hidaya settle inside your body Tell us Hidaya what did you see inside your home supernatural here Is it bad? is it good"? now your awareness....?

Tell us hidaya Did you visibly them? Yea you's mused we see you's worry. Now you aware you must caution You just bought new home abruptly your home been visited by bodies of magic spiritualism. can happen you's get the bad luck from them. From today you's caution you's listen upon us.

I henni; O dear hidaya, I guess you are now fear out to supernatural. Oh, tell me, hidaya? Is it true they are, our husband of friend? I heard they of spiritualism, they very are envious. They yea are envy upon our married envy upon our life If they saw we are eating out We are going out as family as happy family.

I Hidayati; yea according to the saint host and holy holy spirit.

I heard they converses as if about our husband of friend, the first words I heard saint said my husband of friend They been reported us upon Islamic jin wind jin men Iblis wind Iblis women

They live inside Hadis earth, they live inside mujarobat earth tensibly our husband he had promiss thence sudden he broke his promises because we are here. Is this make sense to you henni? therefore you's caution if eating out if you, buy and buy caution

I Hidayati; according toward our guidance I believe them I think garud and banten They're phew information. I did meet with them Yea I saw them. I bit curious but I said They only phew drama. I visible I visit the the old women When she saw me with my husband

I was there I saw the old women she just appearing polite acts yea I saw she bit envious. She visibly me. She dedicates herself she as if dislike me. She as if envious look at me. I am cuddling my husband I kiss my husband I facetious with him front the old women front the old men. I did serious looking upon her upon her husband I did noticed, something that she want from my husband. What Are...? I had no ideas no guessing

I Henni; wow…wow hidaya hurt me. I wish you wasn't blocking my eyes Therefore I can see her, her dedicated, her disappointed Why always you, can notified her Oh I hatred! If you inside me I saw, you always on my forehead You always controlled my eyes my forehead This isn't fare for me

I Hidayati; wow…wow henni you hurt me. Who me did you think? I just or I bad! I did not block your away. My guidance they kept me inside body thus I the first the high seas You's behind me You can't investigation who the old men Who the old women because I of body I the first I spiritual I hidaya. I like supernatural I first saw I first heard

I Hidayati; Oh, yea you's just. We different are spirit, you are soul, you'd easy get hurt easy get emotional because your carried everything as bones as muscles This heavy this emotional thence you create the fight upon me Upon my husband. I'm not like you this hazardous No matter what! I saw he will not tell us the true? that is, his habited he love playing game upon us. Aha henni lets that be…lets that be One day he will cry

I Henni; oh, what do you mean! lets that be? This isn't right? My husband I need him for my children. Oh, why are you easy go off I isn't I love my husband My smart husband I pround I got him. have beautiful children with him Is this make sense to you.

Oh, I tell you my hidaya at first, I isn't like my husband I guess I was young age We fight a lot we swear often. After we got children, I love him more, do you hear me? I don't want to be far from him because "who him" who me" do you hear me? if happen my husband leave me Oh this because if you hidaya.

I Henni; Do you hear me! hidaya if happen that. I be suicide I be shame I shame life here oh hidaya! Yea you's think oh my feeling oh you's thinks where we come from. He come from middle class family cite Raden

We come from rich family Oh yea Who our mother Who our father Oh our father are families They from high militaries also cite Raden militaries You and me yea the same I proud with my parent in law I proud with my families in-law They're Raden I wish one day my sister in law reunion live here.

I Hidayati; wow…wow Henni, you hurt me. Oh, see oh see "Suicide you cite" oh who me did you think? I awareness the soul always, the weak soul I can considerate I can account year by year I think you did not awareness the thing had account year by year. I guess you did not hear god are voices Oh yea oh yea I thought I can see, aren't all the soul can think high can see high as me

Hi Henni, current you love him I let you There out aren't always we sees darkness thereout sudden light the light sign for life We can't turn it off for example the light will come alone abruptly you is bright henni? Thence you question yourself. Why sudden you can forget about him? This because the light and the light changing our life Oh Henni why suicide When time happen You will not remember him

I Henni; Oh, did you seen this happen? I see different than you You seem just and right Oh who me? I only soul Yea I weak soul. I baffling upon you, why are you so strong to let's happen? Should I believe upon you.? Oh, I bit doubtful upon you. You like out to supernatural I anxious What did you saw in our supernatural?

I Henni; Tell me Is it had second person inside our marriage? I visibly you's often sad hi Hidayati why I seen you turned on music thence yourself sing and song I heard I curious ostensibly your voices You's sound broken wish broken love. Aha did you'd seen other desire hoo your music is sound Therefore hurt hurt my heart, tell me? Are you heart weak too? I guess I was not alone.

I Hidayati ; I believe what I believe I saw what I saw. I also was not alone I of guidance, you of guidance. I ready for what happen, I just can't tell you yet, all our worry in dept in our guidance of hand but I promise to you We will be bright You don't fear it wasn't thriller

Hi Henni, People do separate this comment in life. You move on You don't think it, can happen sudden especially the weather here too bright for our husband We are new here, Now let's we enjoy our life here.Oh lucky oh lucky you of me

I henni; aha I still love him you's making the poem I did not saw the sign I only see the sign enthusebe. I visibly I heard host saint they are, will creator blessing healing for our home supernatural. So that bad spiritualism They will leave our home supernatural. This mean he for me he for you. I am looking forward seeing my husband come home

I Hidayati; ah…ah I don't negative I am sorry I saw you sad it you's life it was not my life anymore. It will hurt me too if sudden happen Oh my! I strong I off from the agonize. I was not as you You's weak soul you'll cry aha I don't act that's way. I move on I bright I high I see living saint I see living angel angel As I current I living holy holy spirit they had goal for me I see my bright life I see I lose him I visibly I in the field are nursing I of health care assistance that is it I visible my future life

I henni; hoo you don't wish that I enjoy my home My home my guidance home I was not alone oh good oh good you like supernatural I lucky you go, if you's inside me You's blocking me You's controlled my mind my eyes therefore I can't see what I like to see. I can't hear what I like to hear

I hidayati; aha my soul my weak soul, just think the positive I saw you and me I thought we had different are strength. I spiritual I wind I shape bird; you are soul as dew soul as resurrection soul.

Hi Henni Hail yea this will going on with us. Yea see isn't happen, yet You don't worry O see henni! I visibly today the weather good the weather brigh shall we go

I Henni; yea hidaya! myself today enthusiastic I visibly in map, there had Campbelltown there of Mall It isn't far from here. Hey Hidaya, I like to visibly the mall I saw in map the mall isn't one in Campbelltown There near it I saw Macarthur mall oh lucky oh lucky we are closed live near the cities of mall.

I Hidayati; I see in map there are, Narallen's mall. There are, Camdine's mall tensibly close from Current hill state. Shall we visible, shall we be driving there. I enthusebe I'll taking you there oh my Henni

I Henni; wow Hidaya, I really looking forward going with you. As long as you be the driver. I felt I knew live here. I confess I was not confident driving here or driving there. I think I be merry if you the driver. Oh, shame me.

Henni; Everywhere I saw the traffic I dodder. I visibly the road I dodder to go here or to go there. I visibly the traffic going faster limit wow I weak soul. I easy get dodder. I felt I will be enjoyed going with you Hidaya

Hi Hidaya, I visibly you'd enthusiastic you is, super driver. I can reflection I get to Campbelltown mall or Macarthur mall as rapidly. These massive are malls Therein I believe had culture food had sells. I will seeing there had vary Asian food are sell, shall we go there, we shall see it.

I saw Australia are traffic I saw here and there it seem I saw too busy too fast limit I only body soul, I weak soul. I easy fear driving there aha I cite odd my life here I cite really jocose my life here where is my strength for driving, I felt my enthusebe can sudden up and down

I Hidayati; O my Henni "Who had me" to you wow I am your friend I am, your spiritual. I am your supporter, oh avow it I am your guidance. I born with you I am your strength in your life.

I Hidayati; hi Henni, I think body's soul do need spiritual's friend for yoke for thinks they cite wahoo" you are the lucky you of me. Hey my Henni remember me. I see you are lived here You isn't alone I inside you. I you invoke aha I gives you! body's sock body's surprise aha…?

There up I was, I get you guidance. Hey henni cite it! you aren't alone, I invite many are them. They do They host They light. See! they also your direction See! they your pathways They our healing phooey Henni you's do need them. Hey henni They guidance are healing?

I Henni; hey hidaya you's jocose I cite Oh jocose my life here. Oh, benefit Oh benefit I of them Why sudden yea my dodder rapidly gone? aha my hidaya's bizarre oh bizarre phooey spiritual She get me bright guidance bright shelter who me' oh why I did not miss my husband why I did not think I have husband

Hidayati; oh, certainly can happen! We shall go I enthusebe driving to Campbelltown, this only take us 5 minutes driving there. Today I felt I like eating out, if we now on the morning. Shall we have had breakfast inside City Mall. I think I must ask my guidance. Today we enthuse be going out, eating out I shall ask them

I Henni; I heard you, hidaya yea indeed! you do the right think, certainly you must ask them first. I heard you'd very engaging to them. if you confess you's believe upon them. This mean our life impacting our guidance life. Certainly, report us to them, they must consider where we are going. I believe they perspective isn't the same as us, because they high see they high fly than you hidaya Am I right?

I Hidayati; wow my henni, you do heed my guidance rules. Oh thanks, you mention this to me, this mean you's welcome them coming inside you. They the best direction. They saint host, they holy holy spirit.

I visibly they collaborate with holy holy cross.

They the highest than us. The most knowing, the safety atmosphere Is it bat there? Is it peace there? For instance, if we going to the mall Oh happen can happen "good and bad"

I henni; Yea hoo! it can sudden happen. It can sudden we get mercy. Yea hidaya we both must confess They our belief our believer. They love herbal they love our home ha …ha is this really come through to us They lets us go. I think today I will remember. I must, buy the bible. The bible isn't come alone upon us. Therefore, we must enthusiasm looking toward it and we buy it. I visibly today we will inside the Mall. I believe the bible I had sell in the book shop, shall we see if we there.

I Hidayati; Oh, lucky oh lucky I of henni. You thought just and right than me. your direction, your pathway I feel well indeed. I think I visible my children must of the bible. myself great and I merry I of bible. We shall read, we shall learn, we shall think about it. I feel my mind alert I want reading it. Nevertheless, I must consideration which and which the bible can impact my mind can impact my heart. I think yea my body do need bible blessing.

I Henni; shall I rapidly buy the bible, one for me one for my children. I do think about life. I did asking about life. Is it life creator by the bible? Or is it our life impacting by the bible? I thinks I look forward going to the Campbelltown mall Soon I see one I buy it. I visible upon myself, why sudden I feel I bit weak going there? oh why sudden I lazy dressing well. I Just don't know why? I guest today my desire up and down.

I Hidayati; aha my henni. Did not you's visible our guidance?, they hearing your voices talks I saw they above us They watched us. They smile upon us. They happy you and me, we collaborate together they heard You and I had desire are problem

I Hidayati; hi henni! They above us they heard your grievance. You bit lazy dressing up You bit lazy make up These affected me too Why and Why? I sudden feel this way.? I thought You and me, we need guidance helper I never acts as this I lazy, Ooh my desire abruptly up and down.

I Henni; Oh, my hidaya! Tell the mother host my desire going to Campbelltown abruptly I felt lazy I disappointed I need help Oh what is going on with me? my desire abruptly go out I lazy as if I can't dress myself. I think the invisible thing as if they don't like I talks about bible Am I right

I Henni; oho they heard I grievance I saw the bright coming inside me oho they from above they my holy holy spirit They as nursing spirit but bright, but do They veil dew They aren't one they like mountain sky dew. Now they inside me They own my body They are dressing me well my dedicate myself bright my motivation going high level

I hidayati; aha my body's soul, how happy I am. You and I can collaborate to see it. Now we lookforward going to the mall soon I get there I am seeking the bible I am seeking rosary. I think the rosary can settle our decease inside us

Now shall we both hearing. The voices from our guidance host and holy holy spirit They see high they can say, today if we safe going to the Campbelltown city of Mall.

We saint and holy spirit; yea dear henni yea dear hidaya there up we were, we saw we heard you talks. You are right and just. Yea we saw the weather bright but the supernatural bit hotter. There up we visibly within the earth appeared Hadis of belief on earth they open voices. We aghast the Hadis already above us Therein had jin jin win jin mens of bewhiskeret they aren't one We aghast we are baffling. They had above us they close to our home.

We wonder if people are garud, people are banten They the only your enemies Oh can happen they pray send them here. Ooh what are they up too? The voices the sound, just he and he above They willing to temptation you. as for wasting, temptation for wacky, temptation for accident for scream. Ooh dear henni oh dear hidaya You caution! if you today going out. See magic in jin wind jin jin mens of bewhiskeret They of power.

We saint host; They shape are wind spirit They can going inside people, thence can happen people hatred seeing you. Oh, can happen swear and swear upon you. O dear Hidayati watch your speed limit, can happen. The temptation You get accident Oh dear henni dear hidaya, Caution! with your food buy. Caution If buy, caution eating out. These jin jin wind men of bewhiskeret .They aren't please we live here. This because your husband makes promises upon his families. Therefore, jin jin are wind of bewhiskeret they watched over you

We holy Holy Spirit; Oh dear, henni oh dear Hidayati You don't disappoint the supernatural here seem abruptly aren't good for us. Because your husband he of friend They aren't welcome us live here. They very danger peoples. They people are garud They of power magical They of aiming, as had grief inside our home. I think we must do, the house warmer. Shall we invite all your husband friend to came here Lets we see whose inside them Whose had wind men of bewhiskeret.

We saint host; Shall we set the time? and the date for them Hi henni lets we think further just lived to us Oh today we let you move on going seeing the Mall. If you See bible buy it! If you see insence buy it

I Hidayati the spiritual; Wow .wow my guidance certainly we will buy it. Indeed it important to you. Tell me! are we in hazardous situation here? I hope aren't continue, we get visited by jin wind men of bewhiskeret his shape I dismay.

Henni the soul I enjoy live here I saw the campus I will study again. I see here There I visible the mall There the city See only the beach it takes 1 hours to drive there Wah today you let we go to the mall. Oh, certainly I caution, this only Australia the speed limit is the same as New Zealand.

I Hidayati; I more enthusiastic than my henni my soul. I am baffling why my henni easy dodder live here I curious! I see, she in New Zealand. She very enthusiastic driving She enjoy doing food shopping She enjoy window shopping. I visibly since she arrived here, I saw her appeared changing. I disappointed she virtual demanding on me.

We holy holy spirit; Oh, dear Hidayati We did hear your grievance We did also investigation Why and Why? Wow we visibly it Just the impact we get from hadis earth. We watch full! there up Islamic jin jin wind are magic They jin jin men of whiskered

Angel angel; Jin win jin men of whiskered; They voices above impact your decease, your decease they are spirit inside your body inside your home supernatural . Your decease are voices They as if huhu upon high god. We answer them, the holy cross answer them the angel so answer them. We said don't fear upon jin jin are wind magic wind men of bewhiskeret They only magic wind wind People are garud they pray they send jin wind jin men into our home supernatural They are, huhu thus your body and soul she henni she easy gets dodder

I Hidayati; wow…hurt me wow…i sorry upon my henni she gets hurt get dodder by our decease they are, huhu inside her body. Wow why sudden henni and I get lazy mood. I sudden low motivation. lucky oh lucky I of holy holy spirit what ha! you make us, wah look! You'd dresses us I can see my henni and I We both will look bewitch

I Henni; I visibly the time Oh thanks oh thanks my holy holy spirit I visible my body dedicate beautiful dress beautiful make up Oh benefit I of guidance my motivated down they're help me thus I like going out driving out eating out. I wonder what happen in my supernatural Why and why I sudden laziness why and why my Hidayati her motivated down going to the Mall. I really curious whose rosary make us laziness.

I hidayati; wow we must going Thank you oh thank you, my guidance You make me enthusiastic going I visible myself I bewitch Now I enthusebe Ooh thank you my holy holy spirit. You invoke make us we off now, we go now. Goodbye my guidance I see you soon

We holy holy spirit; Ooh dear henni O dear Hidayati we visible! You are, the beautiful. Goodbye, dear once Watch the time You must going home before midd-day caution see the changing time.

We saint saint; The above earth also changing form after midd-day The changing we saw the form as lion form as tiger form as leopard form They aren't all our enemies but they can give you are bad luck hu Hidayati caution think caution facetious They aren't all faith upon facetious upon converses

I Hidayati; Wow mother are they superstition? we aren't talks about them why hearing we talks wow mother so agonize we live here. tell me mother are they cite Hadis too? Are they cite mujarobat too?

I saint; aha dear Hidayati You smart think You's smart asked Yea the above had culture are belief as lion too as tiger too they of different believer they aren't our enemies but You enemies Hadis magic Hadis of jin jin wind hell fire they are, lion tiger leopard They're attitude very consequences they like backbite they like poison and poison therefore danger for you if you's still out side

I Hidayati; Oh, mother saint, lucky oh lucky mercy of mercy I of you You invoke information indeed I awareness what are life all about

I Henni; yea Hidaya only you's like going to supernatural Oh only me I like going to heaven light. I fear going to supernatural alone I guest we are different spirit We are different roles. Hi Hidayati Are you agree? I guest life all about above life aren't about bibles I heard you converses upon sky sky about life "That is why" I guest our life all about above.

I Hidayati; hi Henni aha you weren't smart thinks the life affected both affecting earth earth sky sky thence creator bibles the bibles the massage all about life as life us from above thence continue the bibles as our guide as our map

I Henni; Aha you and me very interesting gets The way you's think or see True was not they I am I think You'd had more knowledge than me I only can hear I talk it I only can see I considerate it I only can read I delivery it aha what are…?me.

I Hidayati; That is, it…that is me aha time up we go we go now To Campbelltown city.

I Henni; Whoop you's be the driver who me I the passenger I tell you where to go whoop we go

THE CAMPBELLTOWN CITY MALL

I Hidayati I the spiritual; wow no sweat I enjoy driving. aha only take 5 minutes I will get there. I can't wait to see new thing wow hopely all cheaper I believe people said Australia here and there the shopping mall had more cheaper prices compared to New Zealand What are thing cheaper here? I can't wait once we get there.

I henni; oh, yea I enjoy driving with you, I enjoy the perspective I visible There I see the education the campus for mature ages student it will open aha I can enrol in. Wah enthusebe I can study again Thereat I will be meeting with new friend Ooh see! We already get here You is, super driver wah look! I visibly this mall massive mall Oh see magnificent. Oh hidaya! I Shall park the car close to the Mall's doors. Yea easy for me, carrying my food shopping

I the spiritual; wow no problem no sweat, wherever easy for you will easy for me . Yea huhu I the super driver. I the spiritual I think living here, body and soul do weak without me. I meditate. I aghast! I heard my body's soul henni she is, sick inside. The decease been huhu inside my body

Oh I mused Oh I baffled why decease fear upon voices earth on earthy bizarre I heard Soon I get home, I do myself meditate I will inside my body Therein I will see where hurt Is it the ears hurt? is it the heart hurt? I must see if my decease slept or awake, I see if my deceased they fear upon magic jin wind jin men of bewhiskeret

I henni; wow…wow lucky we, we come here on year 1993 wah…what are? Oh, see oh see, there shop I like, there shop I like too. Wow we shall visible, we shall visibly the food court wow… wow! I like here oh see! The culture is food many sell here

I hidayati; Wow yea, lucky oh lucky, I live here, seem you adore all the culture are food. aha we shall we siting here we shall visible we shall choice the food Oh please me, I love eating mie goreng shall you get that for me henni!

I hidayati; Oh, wait lets me see, lets me choice I think noodle soup seem I the most like oh yea I visible I like all the soup

I Henni ; wow that is, lets me choice may. Oh, see I like that, Mie goreng good for me oh see I like that too, red chicken it yea! test nice ooh see that rendang(curry) also delicious. Yea.yea.I bought all.

I hidayati; we shall we eating now thence we move on looking Oh full, filled me

I henni; Yea oh! full filled me. Oh, I felt lazy now, my body bit heavy. Shall we go, where do we go? Shall we walk further there

I Hidayati; wow this shop sell cheaper shoos, shall I buy one I like the colour why here cheaper the white better-looking better design

I Hidayati; Wow yea henni. I like to take it! buy it! enjoy it! I merry I see this shoos design for nursing. Wahoo this my goal I study again. See there! That shop sell clothes wow cheaper, cheaper here I buy some for the children I buy few for us wow see it.

I henni; phooey I waste all my money Now I bit nervous I have to buy the food shopping wow I shame

I hidayati; I heard you, I heard you lets I see our guidance It is true what my guidance said We will get the temptation because the above earth voices upon us wow I see our desire want to buy and buy

I Hidayati; Oh, my guidance hears me, now I anxious Oh I hear I stress and fear! Wow my henni she grievance she worries She only live $50 only to get the food shopping Wow she grievance, she said take my body take my body I feel a shame.

We holy holy spirit; hail dear henni oh dear hidayati! let's we go inside your let we do the food shopping Wow look dear. $50 dollars hail see, we get all we need. why fear why nervous? Cite benedict

I hidaya; yea it is, true what my guidance said. I think yea the voices earth impact I waste our money. Abruptly we broke

Oh, miraculous oh miraculous I of my guidance

They rapidly coming into us they help henni food shopping

I henni; yea I benedict toward my guidance What are, mercy I get from them. I get all what I need for a week hoo I was nervous I did bring enough money abrupt I rapidly broke, hey what did I bought make me quickly broke. I guest this me on faulted

I Hidayati; I said hoo was not your fault, I was fault too. We saw thing are cheaper, we bought it without we think care full. I guess we are, new people here.

I henni ; Aha what are, good friend you are. My shame my nervous abruptly gone I enthusiasm again, looking around.

Yea mercy of mercy I of guidance They did my food shopping I got everything, what I need oh what are, advantage I of them

I Hidayati; I said hi henni! Shall we have walked toward that shop. I visible therein sell the bibles. I visibly! here all the bibles. Oh, why my eyes my heart touch toward one its bible the colour as light blue bible abruptly I heard my holy holy spirit. They voice said buy it, this bible give you give us, the mercy.

I henni; Oh, yea I said, I visibly one too, I saw the design out the cover as sign as angel as sign as earth on earth. I hear my shelter said hail yea henni, you will visible the inspiration. Wow my guidance tell me this a blue bible as if can safe us? Tell me as if I and hidaya we can enter the light of god.

I hidayati; hey henni lucky oh lucky if our wish came through, we get one bible tensibly special one. I saw it I can't wait to read it; I will read it soon once, I get home.

I henni; hail yea henni, yea I did saw this bible We get the mercy the mercy. I saw as bird thence I saw as angel as bright on earth

Wow hidaya, I could not wait to visible inside the bible. I wondering, is this bible can impact my lifer's changing here hoo the colour as if impact my mind my eyes my heart hoo…why is it?

I Hidayati; I believe upon you henni, upon what's you saw. Ah see the benefit inside this bible. The bible can change us of life. Because I like supernatural hey henni! We shall we read, we consideration with us of life. I saw from page to page I read bit, oh yea! May think different. Hey henni, see this one, this bible gives me different perspective. I did open bit abruptly I saw as walking men.

I henni; myself socked Oh who is he? You'd saw. Wow you, I thought, you meet with Jesus. I believe! Yea you are, commotion you like supernatural, now you saw Jesus, Inside bible. I think you! Hidaya, I felt he came into your life.

Wow who me, I shame because I isn't bird, I can't flay like you I can't see invisible thing in supernatural Wow I only body's soul I henni I isn't supernatural soul. I think I do need bible's acknowledge to direction me to supernatural. I like you, Hidayati You is, supernatural spiritualism thus you like supernatural I wasn't like you.

I Hidayati; they're henni, we shall see within these are bible. I saw one or two bibles. These can happen are miraculous. You and I can see thing. I guest thing are can converses toward you or toward me.

I henni; oh, Hidayati yours jocose. Yea oh yea I believe upon you. Am I choice by our guidance to seeing them? I wish I you, I wish you is I am. I like to flay as bird I like supernatural. I like seeing thing too. "Ooh who me" god born me was for the soul to carry all my bones to carry all my muscles I the responsible for my body I the responsible for the obesity ha…ha is this fare?

I Hidayati; wow henni, mean to be that way. I thought, aren't our parent are fault. God are creator body and soul, thence spirit cite spiritual. Hey henni! We must accept it mean we are… that is it! Oh, look at the time! we shall move on looking around wow this mall really massive mall give us tiredness looking around.

I henni, I think I must walk there, looking for rosary where is it sell? hey hidaya, we shall see, to that's shop. We shall go inside! wow hidaya, nothing here nothing there I saw. I saw the time going fast we soon must walk toward the car. Shall we off from here

Oh…Oh why my body feeling dodder, Ooh I sudden get headache hoo my ear is hurt hoo burn I burn

I Hidayati; hoo what is this coming to us. Why my breathing weak. hey what was going on inside me above me. I shall see it oh odd! I heard my ears screamed for help, I heard my eyes screamed The screamed sound about the hot…said the hot wow hurt hurt me I rapidly checked I saw wind cat wind monkey They went inside my body thence hurt my ears hurt my eyes I saw my body's feebly

I Hidayati: I is, spiritual healing I had guidance help. I said hey your black wind, wind cat! Hey, you monkey where are you come from? Why you all hurt my body. my eyes cried my ears screamed by your hotter wind. Hey, you all You'd make my soul unconscious hey …hey answer me! lucky oh lucky I spiritual healing I of my guidance. I said to the bad spirit, hey you all! come, come with me follow me into my home.

hey, you wind cat! wind monkey! what are you enjoyed doing will come to you. Hey, come with me, soon I get home lets you all shower with me You monkey You cat You bird

IHidayati; You all do need good blessing. Hey bad spirit, I am driving home, now you all must following me.

I the spiritual; wahoo only take 5 minute I already get home ouch home sweet home. I got home safe. I get home on time Wow benefit oh benefit I of guidance They were saw, I was carried my body alone Oh yea! heavy load for me. They saw they sorry. They rapidly go inside me. They shower me. they bless me used strong oil used strong salt

Oh, thus my henni my body she rests in bed. My guidance they turn my music on, Abruptly I heard my ears settle my henni my soul she awakes. She like the song She said this is, my song my Indonesian song she said hey hey my hidaya oh leave me alone. I like listening to the song. let's me rest with my song. She said hey hidaya, live my music on, I can pass asleep easy with my music on Oh thence she said home sweet home I like my bedroom.

I Hidayati; wow henni, you don't remember? what was happen inside the mall. Wow I guest this song seem you is, medication. Oh, I aghast. Oh, I baffled who you? who me? I visibly you weren't revenge, toward whose were hurt you, inside the mall. I certainly I curious? Why music ?why the song? my henni she rapidly settles. I still remember! she was screamed she was grievance suffer pain.

I Hidayati; I visibly toward her, I baffled I saw she rapidly forget about what was going on inside the mall. oh, who me, how me? I was not easy forgot it. I visible was, I sorry I heard my ears my eyes grievance hotter, grievance pain hail yea my guidance. It was true what you all said On the morning was, you all described there up had Hadis magic earth therein jin wind jin men Iblis wind Iblis women They of power hazardous They temptation they direction the wind black cat the wind red monkey went inside my body.

We holy holy spirit; Oh, dear hidayati Oh dear yea, Yea we saw jin wind jin men Iblis wind Iblis women They of power they can called bad spirit Therefore we will be leave you alone. We visibly your supernatural our supernatural We been watched we abruptly been followed by the enemies cite jin jin are Hadis earth cite jin jin are mujarobat earth

We saint saint host; Yea dear according god are holy cross They're described they you are enemies They aren't Australian earth on earth of belief. God are holy holy cross said your enemies

They people are garud They people are banten They lived in NSW Sydney.

They of religion cite Islamic magic Hadis They pray upon hadis therein magic jin jin are wind men of whiskered therein magic Iblis Iblis dress in white

People are garud they pray to Islamic magic mujarobat therein women wind dressing in black They pray to mujurobat therein jin jin wind are hell fire shape magic lion magic tiger magic leopard

We saint host; According to holy cross light earth those belief is magic from Hadis from mujarobat They very hazardous They had games above Their games they like backbite us within earth and earth within sky and sky therein all belief lived. This can give us bad luck can happen your goal here difficult to achieve.

We saint saint host; Hail dear hidaya, from now you caution Current they above earth as if they above our roof This because your husband of friend. They pray sends them here

We holy holy spirit; Oh, bizarre saint! We will inside body We shelter her We want not to leave her Yea the Islamic decease inside body make body are dodder and fears.

The decease of thought they as if seen the people are garud Oh they 5 times pray thus 5 time to the magic Hadis earth and the magic mujarobat earth They are coming checking on henni on us.

What Ah thriller, for henni for decease Yea can happen They are going down to living earth going inside our home supernatural. Decease do not like them thus they huhu they emphasize they shoo and shoo the wind wind

We saint host; Oh, caution they wind They pollution We do need 24-hour aircon it must on because they wind wind are asthmatic, they of bewkeret bit polluted ostensibly wind asthmatic wind vomited wind are bad for tummy Oh can happen our soul unsettle. I visibly can happen our body feebly. We shall be leaving our body. Oh, what are option we will used.?

I Hidayati; wow hurt hurt me, my guidance Oh where awry are we doing ? Why sudden, sudden we get mischance?

Oh, wistfully me Yea I baffled Why sudden odd and odd happen here?

We saint host; hail dear Hidayati, oh dear your grievance we wistfully Yea we heard, the holy holy cross light god. They said they will watch full upon these are, peoples.

We saint host; According to the holy cross light god, they said. Those are, peoples often when they pray, when they rosary it answers by Hadis earth answer by the mujarobat earth.

The saint host said; According to holy cross light god, They said if they did pray or rosary on the morning abruptly you been watch full by Hadis earth theren jin jin are wind men of bewhiskeret therein Iblis Iblis wind women dress in white shape If they pray or rosary on afternoon time

You all been watch full by mujorobat earth Inside mujarobat earth had wind magic lion magic wind tiger magic wind leopard they cite jin jin are wind hell fire

I Hidayati; wow what are, socking I heard. why did not, you all investigate before we decide migrated here. Now I remember

Daddy's voices daddy acts He look very emotional, Hev said; we migrated here he did say You follow him! your life defect. I saw daddy spiritual, he out to supernatural He went to my home supernatural His spirit like me.

Hidayati; I visible his shape as bird but he was not bird. I saw him, facetious with holy cross earth He said to me! See there the holy cross of life of me. Therein had holy holy communion saint saint

Hi henni I will get there do deed for me. isn't easy for me to get there oh henni do deed for me that is it only that is bright for me There my father the roman catholic holy cross Ave…ave Maria

You's should sing it he asked hail henni Do deed for me? hail hidaya do need for me. I like to enter holy cross heaven that is it I heard

I henni; I guest once is the ages changing thus his spiritualism often wonder, wondering See his spiritualism ages impact question and question themselves Yea his age affects his spiritualism he fears he regret he minds easy get impact from the above voices thence his spiritualism sudden get stress by the above voices thus he sees different he fears he emotional

I Hidayati; The spiritualism ages he does cry themselves. He asks him selves which way the route He must followed' for example our daddy he is looking for bright heaven. He said it and it He want it but isn't easy to get isn't easy to enter he like his catholic holy cross

We holy holy spirit; Yea hidaya, we guest all, you aren't fault. We tried to investigate his role his life but difficult to find the truth the indeed. Now we awareness we heard. We caution we do better we collaborate we visible which right which wrong We also get to see what are inside the bibles

Islamic magic Hadis magic mujarobat. the power to blind us to distance us away from heaven holy cross heaven moon good moon good star good star. We just can't get the answer right and just. Current we live here; we saw them We aghast We baffled where awry we doing?

I Hidayati; wow I guess my fault too. Once, I heard my husband talks about Sydney hoo my desire up right. I wasn't thought about the consequences Now what are… life I had here? I mused! the bad spirit followed me, thence hurt my body and soul. Oho current I curious! I concern Is this indeed hazardous for my family live here . Ooh we get mischance by supernatural.

We holy holy spirit; Wow did you heard that! The screamed voices from the bedroom. We heard voices go and see hidayati if are we right? The voice seems henni, Oh she our soul she our body's soul. Is she screamed? Why is she screamed?

I Hidayati; ouch yea seems henni, she huhu. I leave her, she was rested in the bedroom with her music on. I checked she was slept. She was hurt and hurt unconscious when we were inside the mall. I saw her suffer in pain; I rapidly own my body I heard her ears were hurt. I heard her eyes were hurts. This when we were, inside the mall. Lucky oh lucky she of me. I saw I rapidly own my body. I rapidly I driven home. After I had blessing shower Thus, I lets her rested. I turned her music this my song. I saw she's settled she's pass to asleep. Wow why now she's hihu?

We holy holy spirit; oh, you were, right. Why is she screamed? she wasn't well yet, she must rest. We did bless your body Yea we saw the bad spirit; they went back up to the earth thence Why she hihu? Yea stays. Stay Hidayati, be with her Yea can happen she had bad sleep bad dream

I Hidayati; Yea I will, I certainly with her. Wah…hoo, what happen to you henni, wow you looked pale. Yea you looked sad. Hey henni describe it to me.

I Henni; wow…wow, I had dream. The dream I saw men of bewkeret cited above me. He talks and he talks thence he changed into differences "look" as look as white wind tiger After that, I felt my body all dodder. Nevertheless, I manage screamed to woken

We holy holy spirit; O dear henni, oh dear lets me own your body oh dear, yea I saw you are, look paled. oho the thriller I felt in this room Wow we cannot believe it. We saw your bedroom clean and tidy. We saw your bed very comfort We wasn't perspective curious. Wow how did he come here.

I Hidayati; wow hurt hurt me. What was, going on here? wah sad…sad me visibly at henni she my soul. Why hurt her, where awry she doing? Wow I smell my bedroom I baffled I so curious? O odd the smell Why the smell as sweet bodies. The smell as animal as never shower. Oho my guidance since I lived here, I did not turn my candle on. I thought live here I isn't necessary I am turning the candle. Wah.yea I visible I can feel! Had thriller…inside my bedroom. I wonder whose send bad spirit come here.

We saint saint host; Oh, dear Oh dear We hurt too. According to holy cross god's light earth on earth. You had enemies live here. They your husband friend. Yea they are, old men with his all family. Yea they are, old women with her all her family . we mused we baffling why sudden they aren't like you live here?

That is, its holy cross said. O dear we think of you hidaya, we visibly you Henni: You are healthy body. You are healthy mind healthy heart . We must caution we aren't leave you alone.

We holy holy spirit; Oh, yea we caution living here we easy we get the temptation. Hey dear hidaya hey dear, henni We are living here we feel bid odd bid bizarre Thereout we been visited by your husband of friend They bodies of spiritualism they out to our home supernatural

They bad temptation hey henni we bless your bed sheet your clothes so that their spiritualism They aren't sleept with you. According to holy cross earth People are garud People are banten they hazardous peoples They are, magic power they pray answer by Hadis by mujarobat of belief They pray isn't answer by the Al Quran they cite peoples are hypocrisy people hypnotism people yore too.

We saint host; Wow well done! Wow well done! Holy holy spirit Thence tell us, where were you all. Henni she was hihu alone inside her bedroom We curious, we saw the sky sky mountain enjoyed visited above. We saw the earth above on your supernatural. We wonder if mujarobat earth if Hadis earth they backbite us to others sky to sky mountain as if there up sky sky are crocodile visited those are, also can sweat henni can sweat hidaya the crocodile they temperature really humidity Now they above us

According to holy cross light The Hadis the mujarobat Earth those are, earth they already backbite us to vary earth to vary sky sky on earth as sky sky are wind dog wind cat wind bird wind snake Ooh what are…nasty are they?

According to holy cross, those are, skies and earth can happen henni get the obesity just to make her ugly dedicate thence they delivery tumour and cancer inside her bones inside her ovary

We holy holy spirit; oh, saint saint host! You all don't offensive or curious about us, we did our job. just and right Now she peace but pale we were, we are up, we aren't far from henni.

We saint saint host; Wow dear these aren't awry you all. We shall meditate, we shall pray to holy cross light. If it is truly the story never ending the people are garud, people are banten they still pray bad sending this earth into our home supernatural. We indeed curious, The Hadis earth the mujarobat earth those are, earth already above us They been malign us upon others are earth earth upon sky sky They giving us aren't healthy living. They are, make our home had wind pollution oh it smell as sweet smell oh humidity as if and as if yea, the smell as animal of spirit never washs

Holy cross and star; It is indeed The old men people are banten the old women people are garud they still pray upon magic Hadis earth upon magic mujarobat. These are, Hadis and mujarobat they do anything for their peoples pray Seem people are garud aren't welcome you live here seem people are banted they aren't welcome you live here aha shall see what we can do aha map them

We holy holy spirit; yea it is truly lord Wow what are, option do you have? This isn't fare for henni isn't for Hidayati

We saint host; yea holy holy spirit, let we sees around! where were the areas feel the thriller. The option we had we sees the blessing are thing We shall choice the smell for her room. We shall choice the blessing for her body.

We holy holy spirit; Ooh how agonize my girl live here seem like, her alive her life here, she will be demanding upon blessing.

We saint host; wow dear holy holy spirit this the only option we can be with her Thereout Many Zion our place our worship they staff aren't awareness we need blessing herbal every day. What Are…clean and clean A for but the tree spirits the bad spirit they can still entering inside zion our place our worship They our bad temptation they very emotional too they easy to punish

We holy holy spirit; yea I agree the place for us has been neglected therein many deceases are colour as black as hot as white as hot

We saint host; Oh yea I agree none are staff heed our need they followed the Bible history only we leave them we lets them think them self Ah see the servant they easy get temptation from black decease from decease aha they are, god they aren't high than us thus holy holy cross they watched full upon Zion supernatural

We angel angel; O dear saint saint host. See ha! The Hadis earth the mujarobat Those are, earth earth been backbiting our girl backbite you to others earth to other sky sky therein crocodile and snakes lived These are, earth They are, above your girl home. They watched upon our home supernatural. We saw, we mused! Those are, earth it signs bad luck for your girl married relationship.

We angel angel; we saw mountain sky sky are Hadis Therein had belief as jin wind jin jin wind pollution shape men of bewhiskeret . These are, skys they, delivery wind men of bewhiskeret delivery wind Iblis Iblis they already inside her bed sheet

We angel angel; We aghast! we saw sky sky are mujarobat. Therein had belief . We curious if the wind falls into your home supernatural wow bad affect bad impact we saw as red wind shape as monkey monkey as red wind shape as cat cat as shape as chicken wind. These are, sky sky we visibly it above, your home kitchen

We holy holy spirit; certainly not, we leave henni alone. Ooh what are, disease they are giving us. Hey dear hidaya, According to holy holy cross light god. Thereout our enemies, earnestly still people are garud, people are banten. They sound revenge's sound rebellious

Why and Why they pray send The sky sky mujarobat here We still waiting for the answer yea mujarobat earth been malign us upon other and others earth earth yea affect Australian are church are earth earth Infect they aren't they truth tellers God are Light and light they watch full them.

We holy holy spirit; Wow thriller here When we were in New Zealand, we pray we meditate up, we did not saw the bad luck. I think we were; we aren't concern about magic We did not visibly those earth on earth appeared I wondered we migrant here to be murder

Wow we did not saw any sign any felt or touch by wind wind are spirit Wow angel angel We mused we baffled wow thriller for our girl live here We visibly earth and earth already watch full upon our home supernatural.

We saint host; lets that be! Too late to be regret too late to be sorry the option we have We lets our girl she moves on living move on enthusebe These are, only our perspective our concern. We deal with that. let them above us we continue the home blessing We also we aren't alone living here.

There up the grief holy holy are cross light god. The grief is moon moon they with us the star star is angel angel they with us.They are, watch full us, they consideration whose us, who's our enemies? Who is our girl? Whose is our girl husband where her sins? Where his sins? aha lucky oh lucky we collaborate with them We aren't alone.

We holy holy spirit; hail dear saint saint host What are, truly your belief, I can visibly my home supernatural bright We visibly her motivation in high level her blood circulation pump well and healthy. Shall we do it more often? Therefore, we saw earth and earth move slowly from us Sky and sky asit move away slowly but they laugh and laugh we still curious upon it

We angel angel; wow dear this aren't yokes the earth move the sky move away yea slowly moves, shall see further, people are garud the old men the old women. They are, heard they sky sky They earth move away from our home They heard they aren't happy They of Hadis earth They of mujarobat earth They thought already curse off by saint saint of belief by holy holy spirit belief They revenge they must the winner toward your girl husband life Now the seeking help seeking assistance to collaborate just to destroy our girl married

We holy holy spirit; Aha what are, the old beech the ugly beech wants from us What are, the cheap women, your girls You told your old men your old women to do magic to get him. Whereat your darling mens? O girl! Are they empty again! oh poor darling he had aren't money to make you's happy oh poor…poor they are, Oh girl! do not your kick your darling upon us We does not want your of men here with us Phooey that is it women are garud did toward mens

We saint host; just aren't only women garut but women banten They the mosh worse. They just the same as women are materialistic so eye money.

We angel angel; women are garud or women are banten They are, parent they like doing magic the aiming for magic to satisfy their girls are rich living. If we acknowledge garud of culture of marriage They very danger people They married culture must of magic They women are wifes caution They are, can separate they husband with their sibling from brother from sister from parent They make our brother. they aren't remembering they are, sister they parent. What are, disappointed the parent but too late to decry. That is, it about women garud about women banten

I henni; wow. Wow what are, all about? I heard my guidance facetious above I felt bright inside my bedroom. Aha hum the smell the smell as if clean my noses. hum am I alive again? Yea since was happen I had bad dream. Occasionally I did fear going to slept thence I did open my bible abruptly I saw shape and shape asif as men oh I shut off my bible I was fear My thought still upon my dream. I called my Hidayati she was, my spiritual helper she was, born with me We had one's body. I said to her, oh please open oh open my bible and read it to me.

I Hidayati; oh, why and why you want me to read the bible? Is it some think curious you? I thought you's look forward to acknowledging it. I remember you'd said; you had vary asked about the bible. I remember you'd asked What was the bible all about? I remember you'd asked. Is it the bible the life for us? Why the bible the history for us ?

I Hidayati I body's spiritual; Oh, dear henni, your self-asked thus you'd don't fear to open it. You's don't fear to reading it. Once you had visible thing thence asking the shape what do you want? yea asking the shape is it life here good for us? Is it life here bad for us?

I henni; Wow you Hidayati you'd remember every think what I asked thence to become serious to you. tell me something what was going on with you. Why can't you share with me ? we both shall read the bible. Hopefully the benefit we can share.

I Hidayati; oho that's what you want? I will but I was not the benefit reader I think I must ask the saint first how to read well it and benefit it. I heard our guidance very curious upon our home supernatural.

Henni; yea hidaya, certainly they curious upon things. Since I had bad dream, they aren't safe leave me alone Oh can happen Happen you get burn. Therefore, I motivated to read this bible, but I fear if it goes wrong.

I Hidayati; yea I agree can happen that's happen We aren't good reading we shall ask our holy holy spirit to help us reading it. Oh, yea I heard our guidance they converse toward the ideas the opinion the atmosphere They going to have house warmer

I henni; yea I think that's good ideas I so look forward seeing whose are, our new friend? Although yea they are, our husband friend lets them see who me? how me? to them thence where awry me?

Ah yea! Whose are they think? How much respect They need from us? I have 4 children I also student I don't have time going visit and visit them They aren't my families. I just thought because these are, they think I am cavalier.

THE HOUSE WARMER

We saint saint host; Oh, dear my Hidayati my henni We do curious upon those are peoples Therefore we will make house warmer shall we inviting your husband of friend came here Lets we meeting face to faces with them Yea lets us choice the day the date for house warmer

I henni; wow my guidance you are, my mother saint my mother magnanimous Yea I look forward having house warmer for my home. I like too inviting my husband are friend I had no curious! Toward them I was not dismay Yea invite them I like them. let's I sees them? let's them sees me?

I Hidayati; I think mother saint, what's henni thought? She no curious to anybody I thought I guest She isn't the person like me. I saw her, she faithful she forgets about their bad so easy

Lucky oh lucky I of her she is amicably soul She forget about the bad happen upon her

Phooey that is me Yea mother I isn't I different. They still in my thought. Oh, soon the house warmer finish. Hail mother, I like supernatural. Hail my holy holy spirit take me to your supernatural. I visible you are high flay than me There up I will visible my birth moon thence you let me live there so that I can visible what people are garud? doing What people are banten? doing toward our life here.

I Hidayati; Hail my holy holy spirit lets my decease they own my body I saw them, they very amicably. They like my henni they help her they also aware I was not Islamic believer.

We holy holy spirit; wow we hurt hurt You are my bright henni she bewitches if you inside her Henni smart if you inside her We like you inside her that is you. Having you inside her Your body bright your body smart Your body enthusiastic wow wistfully us seeing you isn't inside her. She your henni she amicably soul there good about decease there bad about decease They're can make henni's body dodder if they aren't satisfied with henni's life here

I Hidayati; hail my holy holy spirit no..no..I certainly disagree I don't bear to stay inside my body. I born to collaborate with you all thus I cite I spiritual healing I heal my children I heal my body I grade myself I can meeting with you all. I visible mother saint saint I visible holy holy spirit I visible holy angel angel therefore I great my life.

Who me? I wind bird I heaven bird You all teach me right and just Now I can flay high I can tell my henni what to do. but she can't flay She only soul She from foggy soul She to dew soul thence she surrection this because my deed for her. I tell her what make holy cross happy.

I tell her You will take my body to church You meet mother you meet me You meet father Jesus I believe Mary I believe .

Oh, mother Oh mother saint oh hear "who henni, who me" I believe the house warmer indeed important for bad spirit Henni believe the house warmer is for facetious as friend as visitors. I really difference my perspective I curious. Toward they are. Belief and Believer

I rebellious live here I cannot enter my own world my supernatural this my home supernatural there my campus supernatural my children supernatural Oh how disappointed I will not successful spiritual healing I cannot see what is going on inside my children

We saint saint; O indeed my Hidayati House warmer it is important to us too You are new peoples here Whose are? your husband friend? Having house warmer this will help us knowledge who inside them We do curious upon your friend. This need to be done oh soon should be done

You's will be free, free choice You'll peace You will be free going up Yea peace us you leave us We like henni she our bright soul We like your decease They are, your grandmother she dies by magic Iblis Iblis are hell fire. Your father he dies by magic jin jin are animal spirit magic wind lion magic wind leopard

I Hidayati; I was not happy mother I live here, why they nasty to us Where awry us? Whose are they the old men the old women? Why so nasty why haze, they send us aha they really vice they really depravity Yea about times we meet them about time you all acknowledge them who's inside them. Wow Set mother set the date the time for them

HOUSE WARMER

We saint host; Oh, dear my Hidayati soon will see you will learn about people are garud about people are banten how they followed their religion they belief.

I henni; Date Saturday afternoon at 5 pm wahoo I merry I welcome my new friend visiting us Lets they here lets we eat together we yoke together. Aha i be enthusebe I will do the cooking I smart cooks I like my friend happy and enjoyed inside my home

I Hidayati the spiritual; aha I the cleaner I clean my home I bless my bed room I dedicate my flower with vary smell I the cleaner I make my home supernatural bright I bless it with tea tree aha I the art I make my home I provide my wedding photo my family are photos thence I bless it I spray it with jasmine smell. Wow let me dedicate my bedroom aha pink sheet this good for my decease and my henni. The pink it cites desire aha what A life henni have with him.

We holy holy spirit; Oh dear henni they here Oh dear hidaya your enthusiastic your bless our home supernatural you awareness our belief The jasmine we the most likes The jasmine tea we the most like therefore easier for us going inside them Aha they here…they here now.

Henni; hi.hi.you too Thank you for coming lucky oh lucky you all get our address just this. Coming…comin…please yourself where do you like to sit.

Female friend; Thank you henni…we will to sits choice wow lucky oh lucky you of husband he is working hard here wow what he gets for you oh wow this house massive house

I Hidayati I of inside body; Ooh dear henni hurt hurt me Am I the lucky I had him?

The Female friend; Oh, henni oh see…your wedding photos as big wedding is this your mother? is this your father? Oh…oh…

Saint respond; oh. Oh…why are you said that! let's i see who inside you Oh dear inside you had men of bewhiskeret He is the jin jin from Hadis oh dear you of them oh dear his not one he more than one. He been watch full my girl.

The female friends; wow massive your home can I see around wow I never think he will buy home for his wife He had mind to every one as us as us too wow henni you are still the lucky women

I saint; wow dear hurt me why you's decry why him your choice lets me see inside you Oh dear Oh dear the lion the tiger oh from these women are. Oh, dear the snake also from her Her pray answer by magic lion by magic tiger this woman emotional women

The Female; hi henni what are cook? Are you the best cook or are we the best cook Your husband always admire my cooking he said, and he said?

I henni; oh …oh is he been eating your food Oh really is he admire you more.

I Hidayati; ha you henni, she is telling the truth He on and off going into her home This woman magic women She is cite magic food her age old but inside it young gospher cite holy gopher inside it had men of bewhiskeret

I henni I of body; hi hidaya shut off…shut off I tried to be friend upon them You can continue do what you have to do lets me enjoy facetious with them

I hidaya I the spiritual; oh, yea did not you like heed me. all your friend is here They very danger is friend They all cite tiger men tiger women snake women monkey women lion men leopard

Henni Oh what are you think about? I please them, I did not see any wind out from their bodies I guess you bit envy looking upon them. Aha what A yokes I am to you. Hi hidaya do it …do it I let you meditate continue.

The male friend; wow henni, this home big home

Male friend with henni husband; hi you oh you You spoil her aha I thought you hatred seeing her here Wah mercy oh mercy wife you had She is good women She is honest women She is light She is bright ah…ah how did you hurt her Shall we changing you take my wife I have wife

Henni husband respond oh no…oh difficult she choice by my father king(raden) I was not choice her. She choice by my mother queen My mother like her Henni sibling father with my sibling mother they tight this married They in love.

The male friend; Oh…oh that is Oh easy for me Lets me see henni

Hidayati; Oh easy! Out you from your body! tell me What easy? Am I easy women like your wife?

Wah you. Is henni's spiritual. Wow you don't know we secret We are men We deserve to be treat high respect. If women cannot treat, we well We look for better flower I think bright holy flower it better choice for men therefore don't hurt you if mean to be changing mean to change this our life our Australian life here Go…you inside your body

Male friend; wow this massive home. Aha are you bought this aha Really are you bought this aha mean for me and henni

Henni's husband; aha you! Don't yoke front my wife What I did….what I did that was just for fun…just only for yoke I think henni the most faith full waiting for me.

Male friend: Ah you find by me is it find by others that you mosh enjoyed hoo you don't know hoo them can happen henni die

Henni's husband; Oh, I don't believe magic in the name the father the son and the holy spirit henni's alive I down first who me do you think

Female; hi henni's husband aha I see your inwardly you still want your family here

Henni's husband Aha yea sister she the faith full one waiting for me this massive I get here this home she and she design it.

Female friend responds; Oh, yea the old women very aggressive she heard you get together the old men had men for her she out from catholic he is doctoring al Qaeda the old men make you married his girl his garud girl

Henni's husband; Aha them I curious. My parent punishing me if I devoice my wife unless if henni leave me. I never in love with garud women Garud women is the bad women aha she only for fun she only for yoke She is money and money magic and magic

Female friend fortune teller; wow henni massive…home wow henni sad home but you love flower I am happy You hatred all animal they are, animal but you the winner You get everything You happy The holy holy bird fly you back over the sea aha I can't tell you the meaning for that

Henni; oh, stop yokes just enjoy the home enjoy the food

Hidayati; ah you! she did not jocose She tell the truth Her decease is magic decease she can see me Her decease is noisy decease She want to know everything about people are life I watch full upon her

I henni; Oh you. Oh you! stop that I am tired listening toward you triggers

Male friend; hoo good this home hoo delicious these are food hoo who henni she smart smart cooking I guest I am the lucky one

We saint; oh, dear what luck are you aiming too? Who inside you lets me see Wow dear the lion hell fire wow dear inside you had shape as knife inside is it your background belief I saw the decease also wear tradition clothes as wind wind as cloud sky tradition sky wah hoo O lord is this the knife to kill henni body Is this stone to kill henni body

Hidayati oh…oh wow…wow lets me out mother oh too…too agonize hearing his thing inside his body

Female friend; hoo what A home is this? Hoo what A food is this I better cook than this lucky oh lucky I already cook at home

We saint; wah you! Hoo…who you? let's we see who inside you oho this woman she had the same belief have stone have knife have magic lion have glass earth I think it Hadis earth oh see she have magic moon

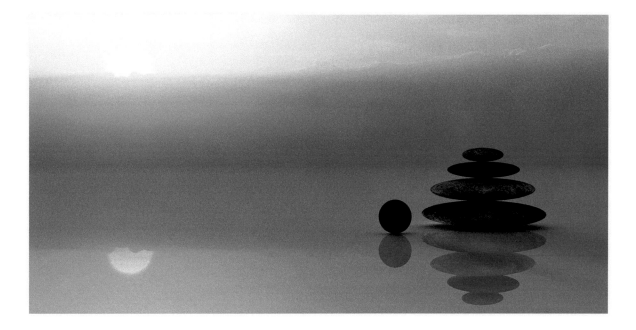

AFTERMATH HOUSE WARMER

Female friend; lucky oh lucky henni your husband own good income here hoo massive home I wish my husband can effort one. We saint; Hail yes you will get one, lets me see whose inside you oh… oh as cat as cat as dog as dog as mountain as sky sky these we called are disease like backbite They mountain inside her white cat called decease called Iblis Iblis They like decry they very envious they spirit like fasting Fasting for die people as if magic fasting

I Hidayati; oh, mother very…very important you let me out Oh mother! I will get hurt living here lets me be with my father lets me be with my children lets me free from here

We saint saint: Hoo what? Benefit of benefit we did house warmer Therefore we caution They very are danger peoples

Oh, whose here? Oh, men of bewhiskeret out from his body he sited into my girl bedroom. Oho what is he up too? Why are you still here hi yea your body went home please followed him?

We saint; Oho who here men of bewhiskeret. Hi, your body already went home why are you sited inside my children bedroom Oh what are you up too?

We saint; whose hectic here Inside our kitchen wow hectic here oh…oh monkey monkey still on our plate on our glass on our cup cup oh dear oh dear henni She will aren't see them They magic magic are monkey They voices are human voices We called them the sinner decease the magic decease

We holy holy spirit; who decease are they? Oh, we see from the old women the old men they people are garud people are banted

We holy holy spirit; oho so hectic around henni make up whose here oho why wind leopard leopard here hey you…hey your bodies already home why are you still here wow henni face will mean for leopard leopard we curious we too curious

I saint; oh, why did I hear voices inside my toilet oh whose there! The toilet supernatural bit humid who inside here

Magic tiger; I of you see you forget about me so rapidly You did see me inside my body

I saint host; Oh, yea you were inside the old women body. The house warmer ending She went home why did not you went home with her.

Magic tiger; Aha saint we choice to live here I like this toilet this always my place Please welcome I live here.

We saint host; oh we…oh we! You aren't right living here We felt aren't healthy Please oh please leave from our toilet We will open the window for you. Please and please leave this area

Magic tiger; oho saint. Did not your awareness What house warmer mean to you. Shall I describe it to you. House warmer mean you'd Gaven us place We take care for it.

We saint; oho magic. You's understand we understand We different are spirit We see spirit like you They don't lived inside the toilet room There are the place Your choice it has up, sky wind sky wind vary colour threat you are belonging.

Magic tiger; oho no…no You was not just You'd said Your direction it was rudest oh saint leave and leave you. This place for us to slept

We saint host; find and find we leave you all. This toilet we seen so darkness shall I candled on shall I spray here

Wow I heard hihu louder thence going up. Now the toilet healthy to used

I Hidayati; Oh, mother saint, is it bad happen inside my home toilet oh now I see bright oh bright Did you bless off the invisible spirit away from my toilet aha lucky oh lucky I of guidance

We holy holy spirit; hail…hail whose voices inside my bathroom hi.hi.wind white magic cat cat your body already went home why are you here? Go go from here on you. Do you want shower with my girl I will shower my girl with you all? Hey hey do not you rudes toward me this my girl home this my home

We White female cat white male cat; wow bright here! Thank you henni thank Hidayati for invite us for your house warmer Now we like your bathroom Your bath better bathroom than us. We shall live here hi saint hi holy spirit We seen we like it here. We saw your towel well washed Oh so bright so bright here. Lucky oh lucky henni of them

I saint we holy spirit; hail dear you all misunderstand the house warmer meaning too We tell you cat and cat house warmer mean You cannot lived inside our home areas to areas

The male cat female cat; oh …oh that's your understanding we are understanding house warmer after we bless, we live here You and we we both collaborate shall you aren't more telling going out from here

We holy holy spirit; Oh .Of. Turned into bizarre wah you all enjoyed it oh don't aghast if do need to clean or to bless thus enjoy the bless thence see the window open welcome oh welcome you back up there

I saint; hail holy holy spirit. Disease ah disease They from body body are friends just caution what are they up too?

We holy holy spirit; oh well oh well saint. Liveit to you. Today we do the cleaning lets we own our girl. Shall we starting oh open all window and door lets them go up to the sky cite sky disease

Oho Dettol good oho the salt good the last the strong incense

I Hidayati; wah…wah very bright here I will own my body thence I will go for shower wow I do like the smell the smell make me lovely desire aha lucky oh lucky I of guidance

Hidayati; wow remember the promises my guidance. After house warmer you all lets me out to my home supernatural I missing my children Wow disappointed I fly up I saw my eyes door close I fly up I saw my ears door close I fly up I saw my forehead also close Why me why me? Why kept me inside my body I don't born to be like this. This really unfair

Henni ; oh, mother oh mother Lets her out from here She the poison for me We fight we fight. I get sick having her inside me

We decease hail mary hail mary lets that be She out from here dodder oh dodder. henni body she is making her Hidaya she jumps, she hihu day by day we hatred hair her voices. Let's her out, lets her see the shape2x the form 2x She like supernatural

I Hidayati; Wow mother I felt Goosebumps inside my bedroom wow I want not sleep there.

We saint host; Hi. Hi dear magic jin wind jin men of bewhiskeret Why are you here Yea we saw you all were inside your body We did visible you all too above the Hadis earth The house warmer ended Your body he went home Why are you still here.

Islamic Jin wind jin men ; hail saint, it this your home? Aha saint is this your home. Why are you invite us here? Did not your awareness house warmer meaning. We like your bedroom Now you must accept who we are. We are here looking after him He is my son; we shelter him since he is moving here. Hail saint are you part of henni. Is she your body if is she just your body Please go back to your body You must accept who him who us This bed good for us good for him, he is, now my son ?

We saint ; Oh, your Islamic jin wind jin men who you talking too? Hey yea we did saw you in Hadis earth tell us. Did not Hadis teach you the manner Who you are talking too. Hey magic jin wind jin men, did not you consideration within your wind and within our wind This room already been blessing for Rahman and for Rahim They husband and wife oh dear leave them alone and forgive them Thence go go back to your body oh mercy I saw your body I saw you are inside him

Jin wind jin men; O dear saint we do what we have too… Your saint saint You all go back to your bodies We tiredness we slept now

We Islamic jin wind we jin men; hi saint saint aha henni's husband his body my son. You clean his sins you clean us.

Hey saint if you aren't happy the ways we are inside him You're take the consequence "do he leave do he stay: whose going to pay the mortgage aha saint no body no women like living saint living faith aha lucky oh lucky the children of mummy. Oh, bad oh bad for my son living saint Happy and happy my son and I we leave her.

We saint; What A sins are you, jin jin men? leave him alone leave her alone She especial for us Will kept them together Don't sins you giving them Shall we bless the room We turn the candles we change our bed sheet hail jin jin men have good slept

We holy holy spirit; hail saint liveit to us we know what we are doing. Aha turned on candles burn the clove oil open all window they know where they are going. Wahoo….lets we all sleep inside our room

Henni; healthy oh healthy I smell the blessing of comfort oh comport I felt my bed sheet aha I felt like going to sleep

Hidayati; Wow now bright my bedroom before I heard argue voices and voices

Oh, benefit oh benefit I of guidance They knows how to curse off bad jin jin wind inside my bed sheet

We saint saint; well dear well dear hopefully they aren't comeback again more less now we knowledge where they are from, we aren't from now curious We caution Hi Hidayati right is you distance you from them They aren't your friend They your enemies. Your amicably to them We see they aren't amicably to you They're very envy to you Ah phooey people are garud here phooey people are banten here.

We holy holy spirit; hail saint " we to be caution" lets we own our body shall we do it our healing shopping Shall we to Camdine city market aha we visible there it had aroma shop had aroma tea shop these shops are we great we merry

I Hidayati; aha I will drive you to get there. I guest at camdine city they had sell aroma coffee. Aroma coffee I edited to it, the coffee very lovely smell My father deceases his love his aroma coffee his enjoyed his aroma coffee

I henni; Yea he was die before daddy He enjoyed drinking coffee with daddy. I heard my spiritual report and report me to them I can't effort aroma coffee.

We spiritualism are garud; Hi saint saint hi holy holy spirit Can we speck to henni spiritual?

We saint; oh, you all comeback here Yea certainly we let her meeting with you as long as your awareness she is, our girl. She isn't free supernatural facetious Please see her…

We spiritualism are garud; Hi Hidayati We disappointed We heard from our belief They're grievance They been curse off by holy holy spirit by holy holy saint saint Hi hidaya tell us How many shelter are you have? aha this is bad for your husband Our of belief they are concern for your husband Hi hidaya did not you awareness? Your husband wants to be free from married.

Hi hidaya he just like us We like new life the old life we will leave thus your husband his spiritual collaborates with us We have our own group supernatural Aha his fun his fun, if we go back to our bodies. We were happy, we sing we song karaoke. We happy wow your saint your holy spirit your holy cross.

They're emphasize him to migrating you're here Oh hidaya believe in us. Dodder oh dodder he was He have too bringing you are here. Hi Hidayati as long as your aware his of our jin jin his of our Iblis Iblis He here he was not alone His of us too Hi hidaya I cares about him the only him I care. I cook for him; my children also love him.

Hidayati; oh, I heard your whispered oh don't said I bright. Wow your information oh hurt me oh happy me. It seems you all like money Yea I can understand You'd been married for so long Your husband aren't loyalty to you They're different than my husband Your husband enjoyed buy and buy Thing and thing.

While you all like money like desire love and love sex and sex While you all like supernatural therein seitan…seitan are games as if changing husband to husband these are normality life for you Phooey spiritualism is garud phooey spiritualism is banten. this wasn't my husband desire hi garud hi banten his more professional than you, you too if he choice you this mean only for food Hi you all, did not know who is he? hi leave him he had his professional women with him Yea believe me, you will get hurts

We spiritualism are garud; Hi Hidayati How rude, you are. Aha is he professional! your blind. He here he temptation every girl aha his cheaper men are he professional? Hi hidaya only with you he as if professional He did say the hatred living saint living holy holy spirit.

Hi hidaya'; that's what you been doing You out from your body thence your temptation all the holy holy spirit to guide him for you Your temptation holy holy saint to guide him for you this isn't fare

aha hidaya his of lady professional aha Yea us and us too. Aha hidaya do not blind us We awareness you did not love him Oh you don't blind us We saw you's broken heart tell us. Are its good men thereat hidaya? You just distance off from him Tell your henni Accept and accept what are come to you. Mischance and mischance do happen in life Hi hidaya tell henni lets him go and go

I Hidayati; aha phooey magic spiritualism is garud Magic spiritualism are banten You all must believe upon me Aha you all will get hurt Wow did you all acknowledge Where his parent back grown are? Wow who his? who me? We are balance We are from level as Raden (king) we high level choices, phooey we are different than magic spiritualism are garud Than magic spiritualism are banten

We spiritualism are garud; Wow he lives here you live here You can't use title raden hoo who him? hoo who you? he loves bed, bed us He isn't choice high he ate with us. He is us He isn't Raden he leaves Raden Hi…hidaya to you his Raden You can't cite his Raden here We cite our men. Our spiritualism Our superstition He collaborate with us We his families

Hi Hidaya, heed our sentences if the saint saint if the holy holy spirit isn't happy seeing our belief live inside your home, we rebellious his of us Henni must accept life do happen separate Henni must accept life do happen devoice see can happen and happen. This really henni's faulted why live him too long with us Here his lonely…we there for him He miss his children My children there for him.

I Hidayati; phooey…phooey magic as you You like my husband Seem my husband the only men had money here to do your food shopping Wow I sorry You all aren't get him Thereat professional lady waiting for him wah why don't you believe me You all will aghast You all will disappointed You will see I and henni fly and fly we happy we merry

We spiritualism are garud; Hi hidaya hi smart you with your game You see hidaya once you let this happen, you'd hurt us You's comeback here Henni will be disable Henni will be end We make this because your phew are game. Hi hidaya You will get hurt You lose the case the justice never ending the fortune all gone This because your games You took his love away from us You get him women you's choice We rebellious We will never let your body happy

I Hidayati; Phooey women are garud Do not believe upon belief as magic lion The lion's magic cannot put your heart together I hidaya I holy spiritual I also of guidance believe in me, Only we can put his heart to you We dislike played game We only like the fact the clear the even the ending. Phooey we are.

We spiritualism are garud; hoo you do you thought this funny Yea we believe you You only like to hurt…hurt us We so hidaya we love his money thus we guide your body she make sure! she wasn't waste his money

I Hidayati; Aha magic and magic Phooey women are garud believe in me, his my husband Henni make him his nothing live in the bank his card empty his bank with henni because he's worry henni's leave him hi spiritualism are garud You waste your time waiting for him It better lets henni have him His of henni Henni of him Oh don't hurt oh don't shame if you lose in supernatural with me

We spiritualism are garud; Yea hidaya yea phooey we women are garud We lose We aren't yet. Hi hidaya but we see henni's lose the case the justice We see you are fly cry and cry mummy and daddy They're dodder thinks for your future goal

Yea hidaya we are here to warn henni to lets our belief They like your home They will take care toward henni They will take care toward the children Your children will be my children If your saint your holy spirit they still blessing your home thus the havac will soon happen upon henni.

I the lord I Holy cross light; hail saint watched full upon your girl health. There at the old men the old women They people are garud. They had aiming to separate her, from her husband thence they aiming to kill her. Caution you with your girl henni with her spiritual hidayati. Hail saint hail holy spirit teach her your roles of belief. Teach her your roles as believer.

She must heed, oh I see in few years up, can happen. Happen your girl feebly ill and illness. Therefore, hail saint hail holy spirit teaches her your belief your blessing. We see the old men and the old women. They very power to kill henni. They just envious because she of good guidance her guidance pious than them We see they want to temptation henni They seen, they can't because henni of host guidance. Well teach saint well teach Henni of power to curse off them.

I the lord I holy cross; I hail sain hail holy spirit, yea heed. Jin wind jin men of bewhiskeret. They backbite the saint the holy spirit toward their bodies to the old men to the old women. Jin wind jin men said the saint the holy spirit They the winner heni and her husband they together again. Therefore, People are garud the old men the old women They're hatred they're shame thence they trigger Further they are making wish as magic wish. They collaborate with jin win jin men they from Hadis they from mujarobat "the wish just to kill"

There are 5 wish supernatural are methods How to kill henni and hidayati.The old men the old women. They have 5 method of power which are thing, they used magic lion magic tiger magic leopard for cancer for tumour for high fever for BSL for MRA

The old men his of magic stone his power the stone used for damage teeth for damage bones the stone used for damage kidney used for damage head thus both're get magic headache fever vomiting sore tummy thence weak

The old women she of magic bottle the bottle used for damage muscles.

The knife (Kris)used for damage joint joint for damage skull inside the brain Knife used for damage bones

They used smoke for magic spiritualism the spiritualism they can going inside body to do suicide to do wacky to get accident

AFTERMATH HOUSE WARMER

They used magic coffee to get spiritualism so that spiritualism they can bring seitan grief inside body to damage heart to damage mind. Hail saint hail holy holy spirit You all-star your teaching knowledge as belief as religion for henni for hidayati

I henni; the night before I went to bed. I had my night shower after I finished shower. I dried myself I used my white bright towel. Wow I aghast why my towel makes my body tight and tight thence I weak I tiredness thence my love desire down. Myself thought I abnormal this rare happen to me. I sorry upon my husband My desire was slept and tired. Myself also grievance why and why? Happen this way. I called my spiritual I was facetious with her I said hail my Hidayati funny was funny my sexual desire down for my husband I felt my body muscles so tight and tight I felt so laziness Oh help me? What was wrong with me, this feeling happens after I used my white towel

I Hidayati; Wow henni, I did see I aghast too Therein i heard in my bathroom voices and voices as if talks. I see the shape as white female and male wind cat cat They voices as human voices as our friend they are, mother and father voices I heard our guidance talks they very curious toward it as invisible things Lets, I informed them They must knowing.

I henni; Oh, hidaya please do it for me lets them know! I felt I am too laziness I need you to carry my bones and my muscles

I Hidayati; Oh, dear O dear my holy holy spirit I curious henni of concern and worry She was not well from last night and current she appeared worse She had shower last night She used her white towel thence her sexual desire down toward her husband. On the night I was not with her I was not wished to sleep with my husband. I see his face he was not him; he was not the men that I love His spiritual was not inside him therefore last night I ignore him.

I saint we holy holy spirit; Oh, dear henni oh dear hidaya! We forget to bless your bath room Oh dear aftermath house warmer Yea all bodies they went home but bodies of belief They lived here They choice the areas and thing for them They live around your things They're we cite human are magic disease They yea white wind foggy female and male cat cat They can do bad, they can do good hi henni, Shall we bless your towel shall we bless your body. Now you must watch full eating rice They also cite rice disease

AFTERMATH HOUSE WARMER

I henni; Oh, awful Oh awful I felt this was not fare for me. I miss my husband I can see he miss me thence I was too tired until current I felt heavy to walked Please my guidance bless me oh bless me . Please my spiritual You's take my body You's own my body Y

I Henni; I woken on the morning I went to my toilet suddenly I felt myself as if my ovary hot my colon hot my urine hots my back hot. I called to my spiritual I said why I felt my bed different Oh only me and my husband slept inside my bed sheet Wow why strange why I felt my body abruptly unhealthy? Oh, who was in my home supernatural? She or He Are they went inside me? Are they going inside my bed sheet? oh…oh. whose shape slept with me. I called to my spiritual Hi hidaya help me? why and why I felt this way oh rare happen to me Wow helps me? help me hidaya.

I Hidayati; wow again and again I heard. Never ending. wow I curious O back hots. I curious colon fever, urine fever ?. Why only back middle bone hot why isn't all body hot. Hoo I serious curious! Hi henni shall you open your bowl, lets me own my body oho yours poo shape lion as if tiger too. I do fell hot in the colon Lets I inform our holy holy spirit. Oh dear…dear my guidance again and again henni she gets back luck She isn't healthy in some areas inside her body as like as fire

We holy holy spirit; oh again! Oh, yea seem magic coming here we are wondering if the old men the old women. If they still pray magic pray magic rosary thence sending mujarobat of belief into your bedroom

We Angel angel; hail holy holy spirit yea the old women with old men they still aren't satisfied You all the winner brought them back together. They very trigger toward it. They do any think to defect this married. Just see how strong your belief to fight their fire. They rebellious henni should not be here If henni and Hidayati she isn't leaving the house thus she ill and dying inside this house.

We saint; Oh, dying oh phew! our girl good girl she was not like their women's. Certainly, they trigger they shame toward themselves. Hail yea don't worry we faith we wind Lets we bless her

Henni; mother oh mother Holy spirit of holy spirit Your invoke I felt different why sudden my body settle I enthusiastic my desire I miss my husband sad oh sad he was not here oh sad he was in Brisbane Oh mother oh mother saint Wow I fear to seeing my white towel hi hidaya can you kept my white tower away from me!

I Hidayati; hi.hi.henni don't be like child acts. Here I am, mother, holy spirit They're teach me the healing sites. I confident to heal you. You don't worry! if that happen again You be the winner to have him in bed

Henni; Aha You don't be jocose. Your husband too! Do something for him, help him thinks. Wow instead you like distance away from him Wow hurt me because you were not desire supporter for me. Instead you leave me alone because you distance from me thus bad spirit slept within us. Hi hidaya tell me What make you's hatred upon him?

I Hidayati; wow…wow henni. When he comeback from work or he came back from Brisbane or Queensland His isn't his His I saw different a person See oh see I saw in him he had two or three person as spiritualism thus his desire toward me as if break up but toward you isn't yet.

Henni; Oho hidaya! I am really sorry but You's must think we have children with him Oh hidaya, you's think "word for breakup" isn't in our family roles. We had culture in our tradition we of family name I believe our mother her desire now merry If she hear your hatred upon him, she will cry and cry She will sad and sad Hi hidaya tell me did not you think who our mother? Never in her role, her perspective she always thinks we the best married we create good example toward our sibling sister and brother

I Hidayati; oh, see oh see I wish you is me We can fly up together the above we are. We can see bad we can see good about him role in felt to field Wow broke oh broken I broken love broken desire.

Henni: Wow I cry I cry oh seem You isn't forgiving him. Yea You leave above Wow comeback inside me I lets you listen to your music

Hidayati; oh, dear henni you's amicably I shall I... I should….?aha I choice my song

I henni; broke oh broke me listening of you'd music. I wish the song you'd choice will has affected me into fire mood. Tensibly your song affected me sadness affected me weak affected confused

Hidayati; Aha you can't say my song affected you always You can say my song will impact our life changing aha guest it? Hi henni i must leave you wah enjoy the home you seem healthy after I sing my song to you

Henni; Yea.you.where you too going

Hidayati; Aha you were not alone inside body. Ha.ah seem today our decease all settle They slept well inside our body I guest today our home supernatural as if looked peace. My breath I heard settle and bright Goodbye my henni…Will be soon I be with you.

We saint saint ; rest oh rest we inside our bodies wow oh wow so bright my soul my henni. Healthy oh healthy my soul my henni. Rest oh rest you's my henni oh let we oh let we…lets we own your body hail, shall we? Where…where it? Our bible shall we create worship for henni for hidayati to safe her from fighting fire We are the lord the true god the true god with us light from light.

We holy holy spirit; hail yea saint hail yea saint Your teaching Your rosary your pray henni and hidaya She will get the power of god She will see the trough Jesus (Isaac) the trough Mary (Mariam) wow the almighty will collaborate with us we aren't alone thence….. shall we creator the blessing. Oh, see heaven moon heaven sun heaven star They are making creates the tea tree bad for magic spiritualism The Dettol this bad for magic lion magic tiger the clove oil this bad for magic spiritualism aha gone you all for ever

We holy holy spirit; Shall we creates the nutrition the fluid for henni for Hidayati we will see the meat and fish plus super vege as lemon, ginger and turmeric these are mixture drink this good for her. Oho the cake we are decreasing the bread we are decreasing the cheese we are decreasing we choice our fruit avocado pineple English pear that is it for today

Henni on Friday afternoon I was meeting with my college inside MacArthur mall We were sited inside the food court we ate mac Donald after that my college and I we sited we been facetious about our task wow at sudden I felt as knife on my foot the knife as if making hold into my food joint the first I ignorant thence I have to stand and walks wow happen I was limping and pain I screamed called my spiritual for help I said hidaya take my body own my body I was in pain and tell me who did this toward me.

I hidayati; aha what now?

Henni; oh, hidayati you don't say that Your grievance to help me wow looked upon me my foot really hurt

I hidayati;wah henni!yea I heard hectic around you as if supernatural The magic spiritualism They're holding magic knife shall I called above toward my guidance oh dear…oh dear my guidance look and look the spiritualism they holding magic knife toward henni Oh see henni, she as if she get attacked by spiritualism oh my guidance shoo them shoo them.

We holy holy spirit; oh, dear henni oh awful henni by them. Today afternoon seem superstition afternoon as if bad magic easy touch upon human oh looked there had vary shape are spiritualism in mall supernatural see within them, they your enemies

We angel angel; hail holy spirit hail saint. The old men the old women phooey garud phooey banten phooey they're Islamic believer We saw they're pray They aren't like others Islamic peoples

They ostensibly they're magic Hadis We see today they said rosary They're rosary just to hurt henni. We heard they still decry why holy saint holy spirit blessing henni and her husband They decry and they rebellious They aren't like henni together with her husband hail saint hail holy spirit what are mischance they're wish for henni.

I saint I holy spirit; thanks angel for you invoke oh dear henni lets we see your foot lets we bless it at home.

I henni; oh, you are the miraculous You're coming inside me Wow I less in pain you're coming inside me I was not unconcious oh bless me oh bless me oh take me home oh take me home.

I hidayati; lucky oh lucky I of guidance I was not alone to heal my henni hail my guidance it all truly they're will not leave henni's alone I sorry to her but henni isn't understand all this. Oh, mother saint I had enough see him his not his because his my henni torment my agonized when is she going to be awareness all the azardous here. Wow mother saint I cry if you hurt, I said if you're hurt You do so much for us Especially my holy holy spirit, they my guide they're work hard for henni for me shall we leave him

We saint saint; oh, dear henni it is hazardous they whispered they wish Especially spiritualism are garud spiritualism are banten They hazardous people are here they believe magic Hadis they believe magic mujarobat the seem yea never-ending revenge

We holy holy spirit; hail saint we do not surrender to soon if we do, they'll laugh upon us They're thought we were wrong upon this her married. Hail saint my girl henni she concern toward the children happiness The children they do love him his also good for the children aha saint what are magic miraculous The magic they're can make him forget toward his children they can make the children forget toward him phooey oh phoey women are garud women are banten

We saint saint ;We see we will see how much henni hurt by their magic method We do our best to bless her to bless her home We do it we sorry for our children we won't surrender we seeking strong justice This isn't henni faulted just him get mix to the wrong family The families are lion tiger leopard jin wind jin men Iblis wind Iblis women as women cat cat dog dog bird bird whose They are, like doing magic

I Henni; wow such as enthusebe day to day wahoo today I be at university I have lecture on the morning The topic I really like as about nursing culture I was focused listening toward my teacher's lecture Sudden I felt like stone sited on my head abruptly I get strong headache the headache become hot on my head oh I just can't focused listening to my teacher's lecture

I called my spiritual she rapidly own my body she said wait who I seen on your head Oh the stone the black stone inside the stone had old men of bewhiskeret with his black stick as shape as snake stick sited on our head He make the sound as took…took as nock…nock I though this wasn't only stone this as spirit as seitan spirit oh lets I rapidly informing our guidance

I Hidayati; wow suffer henni wow awful henni. Hi henni I help you shall we going home shall you rapidly get the drink instead . I did not hear her voices I guest happen her unconscious. Nevertheless, I own my body I get my drink the water I drink I abruptly I vomited I called my guidance. They watch me they heard me I can felt they followed me aha I am driving home I see I survive I arrive home I get home safe

I saint saint I holy spirit; oh, henni oh hidaya you's looked awful lets we…lets we own your body lets we bless your foot with water salt

I Hidayati; wow I benediction I of guidance my breath star and star came back upon me thank you my guidance my breathing you invoke earnestly benefit for me my tummy also slowly settles

I saint I holy spirit; wow dear tear us henni you are amicably why they are, always bad upon you. Ooh see all we can't forgive them oh hurt my girl oh.oh.awful my girl they make

Angel angel; the magic old men the magic old women. Phooey People are garud People are banten They envious upon henni's goal Especially they of young spiritualism They're working hard but never happy at home. They are, fight and fight We see they often happen they're hatred and hatred The spiritualism they miss henni's husband They miss what they were doing before Therefore they of body soul they make strong rosary to break henni's married The rosary answer by mujarobat earth oh bizarre oh bizarre

Angel angel; hail saint hail holy spirit caution today Thursday night we heard magic lion magic tiger they hihu upon they of spiritualism We heard the lion and tiger emphasize upon spiritualism the lion the tiger. They want all the spiritualism They must holding their magic knife. Magic Lion magic tiger emphasize they must walk toward henni's home supernatural thence Thursday night henni should be kill. Lion and tiger emphasize upon spiritualism henni's ears must kill henni's face must kill henni's heart must kill henni's forehead must defect henni ovary must kill henni's head must kill make her wacky make her stupid Defect her torment her

We saint saint; again and again oh never ending they coming here thus unfair for henni and hidaya we heard our girl tonight going out seeing her friend as mother night as mother party Thank you angel for your invoke we will thinks the safety for her tonight oh tell me what time are they doing the magic

We angel angel ; oh, dear oh dear will be late night within 1 am or 2 am

We saint we holy spirit; oh…hue…hail dear we will see We just inform St Raphael St Gabriel St Michael

Holy holy cross; well done saint well done holy holy spirit They job are these. If we aren't here Be smart seeking them for helps

Never…never let magic lion magic tiger They the winner kill my girl kill children

Henni; what A enjoy night tonight the party over we also tiredness oh full…filled our tummy the food all delicious oh home sweet home my home tonight so bright the smell also bewitches oh slept me oh slept me I am looking forward for tomorrow oh good night hidaya

I Hidayati: oh, good night henni oh stress me saw you in the part Yea good night henni see you tomorrow. Oh, mother oh mother see she is back I heard angel angel above laughed upon her that is it henni. mother! she isn't remembering the pain. lucky oh lucky my guidance they can engaging with the angel angel.

We saint; oh, dear hidaya she is just like Rahim therefore current she bad luck many hurt in her asit the hurt coming and go eventually she my bright one Only she can stop can end her enemies "aha will see" will happen?

We holy holy spirit; oh, dear saint oh saint lucky oh lucky all the spiritualism is garud the spiritualism are banten They fear upon St Raphael earth St Gabriel earth St Michael earth They all leave from the magic knife They all go back upon their bodies

Angel angel; hail saint hail holy spirit you all still caution the old men of young spiritualism the old women of young spiritualism they are garud they are banten they indeed wishing henni's must devoice thence They said and They said pray upon mujarobat earth of magic belief as lion as tiger

I Hidayati. oh, mother oh angel I did meeting with the spiritualism I said upon them they aren't the lucky to have my husband oh mother the holy holy spirit already let me see my husband he had wedding again why and why they don't believe in me

We holy holy spirit; oh, dear hidaya do not you lets henni awareness this lets god are light star god are light holy cross lets them judge it henni and her husband inside their holy court there are gate there are date there are ending years

I Hidayati; Tell me my guidance who will deal with that oh make sure was not me I fear I fear whose guide henni

We holy holy spirit; oh, us oh us oh holy cross oh holy cross hi hidaya will isn't now will happen
We saint saint; Oh, dear oh dear seem this year the earth funny earth Ooh the June the bad
month the sad month. How they are doing it?

I Hidayati; oh mother oh mother henni and her husband ate pork often ate red pork They cite delicious pork oh mother oh mother my decease as my father and I We drinking coffee often it really satisfied us Tell me mother Are these make henni had bad luck this year?

We saint saint; Oh, seem yea by 13 June 1995 We will see Oh what are they up too? They already going inside your body oh as if the fire earth already in your blood The Islamic magic lion also already in your blood are heart Hail lord don't take her she mother magnanimous Oh lord don't take her she mother the faith full Oh lord don't take her she is will be mother charity O lord she is will be meeting with you light and light . Oh lord she is will be meeting with Jesus's host She is will be meeting with mary's host Oh lord she is will be resurrection

Holy holy cross; hail saint hail holy spirit goes…go…checked her health checked his health How bad is she? How bad is he?

We holy holy spirit; O lord we certainly we will. We heard henni lately she grievance lazy and lazy slept and slept She refuse pick up the kid she grievance tired and tired thus hidaya and we own her of body We just cannot leave her

We holy holy spirit; therein some areas inside her body the temperature bit hotter O lord we certainly must checking her seriously We will take care her today to near Doctor at Campbelltown we asked for blood test Wow lord oh saint we tear henni her blood she is positive leukemia according to doctor she must rapidly stay checked to hospital Liverpool

Holy holy spirit; oh, awful us oh guilty me, where are we? Oh, awful us why and why this happen is its magic rosary making her hotter is it magic pray making her hotter wah garud wah banten nasty oh nasty people are garud people are banten phooey magic magic

We angel angel; oh dear. Oh dear holy holy spirit isn't time yet her going to holy cross her body must entering to holy church thereat she see vary mercy indeed she see how to charities she see the servant the priest she enjoyed the worship she alive within and within 3 month she recovery with catholic marry rosary

We saint saint; oh dear oh dear hidaya you don't fear you don't cry read our teaching pray our teaching bibles Do it hidaya thence read and read your bibles thence drink and drink our roses water drink and drink our green vegetables water within then she comeback hi hidaya henni already rested inside holy cross She will be back into your body hi hidaya you and your body we move on we alive lets she go lets she live with holy cross he took her Your soul resting in holy cross light.

Magic spiritualism; hi henni you don't awake you slept for ever lets we take care of your children hi henni now you awareness who we who you we lost beginning we winner at end thence we saw your grief we bright again we said good bye for ever current you awareness who we who you? Goodbye henni…will soon your children they will following thence you leave him alone

I Hidayati; aha phooey magic is garud phooey magic banten who you talk too hi your spiritualism! You're see me Hi I see you all. I inside my body I of body. Hi carefully you! My soul henni she had above you She watched you. My soul henni! she is bad soul above you she watches over you.

Spiritual are garud; wow what is going on with our belief the mujarobat they cannot kill her Hi bodies' souls henni still alive her spiritual now own her body wow we did hear her voices above us Hi our body body are souls Oh rosary oh rosary for us Oh fasting oh fasting for us Henni she still alive just to make sure called her husband at work and asked how henni doing?

Hadis tiger mujarobat tiger ; hail my spiritualism do not you all disappointed yea she wasn't die Hoo yea we lucky with others we able to kill them to defect them but with Henni body's soul she different she uneasy She had many holy holy spirit in the heart in the muscles She had saint saint spirit in her for head She had holy cross light holy cross bright on the head. Aha our spiritualism what good think we have done We did defect her financial the house soon for sell She lose him eventually devoice happen can happen. Oho don't disappointed our spiritualism henni's spiritual she own her body Yea she isn't alone we see spiritualism she fly back to new Zealand she lose the case That is why she own her body aha we saw she will wasn't able out to supernatural that benefit for all us.

We spiritualism are garud; Oho tiger tiger (lord lord) dodder oh dodder we felt if we are going back into our bodies are souls. Henni're lord lord will decry us oho how bad our sins? Oho what're decry what're rebellious we will get from henni're lord lord

Seitan seitan are garud; Oh you all don't dismay Catholic are belief they weak believe We the most strong belief than them If they're rebellious if they're revenge if they're decry we called our fire earth our sky fire these are, can have them aha Catholic's henni they aren't have magic fire earth They aren't have magic sky fire but we had it…only we had above

We spiritualism are garud; aha seitan you invoke it does faith us it does give us enthusiastic therefore we aren't dodder any more

Tear oh tear my mother my daddy They heard what're happen to me I said to my mother just pray yea doctor said to me I had short life I must stay at liver poor hospital aha mum…mum I refuse I said to all the staff are nurses I will comeback in three month I do my healing first lucky oh lucky they lets me stay home they respect my belief My mother said I pray for you. I will be with you I will book ticket I fly there

Worry oh worry my sibling They're cried and cried wow I mused my sibling eventually they all reunion to Australia According to my mother soul I really looked as death body She was slept with me she also healing but she different healing than me I heard her spiritualism she out from her body She was inside my home supernatural thence I heard saw she cried upon tiger tiger upon men of bewhiskeret she asked forgive my girl soul where is she? where is she? oho take my soul hurt me but isn't henni to be hurt. She had 4 children they're adore they're mother

Hadis tiger mujarobat tiger; aha this accept life Life had test for your girl Why your daughter married him His unclean men he sins men aha from the marrieds' beginning He always lies upon his wife This men had many jin jin are fire inside him This bad for your girl Here he slept upon wife to wife oh why and why your daughter reunion him thus we all emotional we saw wife and wife here They ready to leave their husband Just for him did not you awareness your daughter born she back for god therefore she must married holy really holy men that knowing who is she?

I saw my mother bow and bow Oho forgive me forgive belief lets her alive oh belief sorry to see her children oho what are future my grandchildren alive without henni

Hadis tiger mujarobat tiger; oho we tell you! where is she? . she was with us Now she was above with holy cross

I Hidayati; oho I saw my mother acts to Anne's nurse she asif like pray her both hand point it above then she said Anne nurse she'd holy cross nurse She love her She like her since she was toddler ages She took her away from us. I heard she talk Oho daddy you's my father in law You is, holy cross I saw my mother bow and bow to my daddy holy cross

I Hidayati; She said take me take me but return henni to her body. I heard holy cross said she alive She henni's spiritual she's own her body soon she be in new Zealand I saw my mother looked upon me but appeared confuse I saw she's thinks alone I heard her voice how…how…she can alive one, She should be two thence she come close to me she said Oh my darling henni Oh my darling one is, I adore you since you first born You make mistaken live here We were wrong about him O my darling henni followed what daddy's said You must go back with me do not sad! let's that be! sell…sell everything further I heard holy cross emphasize upon my mother.

Holy cross; hail henni's mother! did not you listen to me this men he was sins here hail henni mother believe in me! take…take your daughter home to New Zealand thereat she's alive Oh here on 1998 will see she will be in court she the winner she get the children you's sell their home aha On 1999 she'll devoice him aha on 2000 this good year for you all Oh you's take her back to New Zealand aha she my daughter aha She will light aha She my daughter aha she will bright aha she of job ha there it she success than her husband My emphasize whoever is he with…He'll never happy. He also will not come back to catholic if he will he die.

I Hidayati; I saw my mother cry and bow I heard her voice said oh holy cross oh daddy oh my father in law happy I am hearing henni alive again I will…I will taking my daughter home thence I saw she live inside me I saw she collaborate but she bow and bow to Saint Mary Mac Killop her's soul and her's spiritual My mother bow She said Oh Mary oh Mary forgive My daughter sins oh Mary oh Mary help us help us

I Hidayati; I said to my mother aha mother I am different spiritual than Henni. Oh, mother Henni is, the soul Now! I of body I can see you in supernatural but henni can't see you in supernatural if she comeback into my body. Which and which do your choice within us? Oho I saw my mother cry and cry She mused! she saw all the decease They were hurt and hurt by the hotter wind wind are earth I saw she very emotional. She makes herself enthusiastic to sell and to sell wahoo we all are going back to New Zealand I said Home sweet home I live with daddy and mummy happy….happy again